PEN AMERICA

Published by PEN America,
an affiliate of PEN International,
the worldwide association of writers
working to advance literature
and defend free expression.

www.pen.org/pen-america-journal

PEN America: A Journal for Writers and Readers
Issue 19: Hauntings

PEN American Center
588 Broadway, Suite 303
New York, NY 10012

This issue is made possible by the generous funding of The Lillian Goldman Charitable Trust.

Printed in the United States of America by McNaughton and Gunn.

Postmaster: Send address changes to *PEN America*, 588 Broadway, Suite 303, New York, NY 10012.

Email: journal@pen.org
Phone: (646) 779-4816

COVER ART
Images courtesy of Steven Bley

ISBN: 0-934638-55-1
ISSN: 1536-0261

PEN AMERICA

19 | HAUNTINGS

EDITOR
M Mark

ASSOCIATE EDITOR
Laura Swearingen-Steadwell

COPYEDITOR
Loren Noveck

EDITORIAL INTERNS
Sabrina Diaz
Logan Hill
Elena Nicolaou
Madeline Pages
Nonzamo Reid
Daniela Spencer
Juliany Taveras
Bridget Whitfield

LAYOUT/ART EDITOR
Angela Davis Fegan

CONTENTS

PHOTOGRAPHS BY STEVEN BLEY

HAUNTINGS: A FORUM

For the forum in this issue, we asked writers:

Who or what haunts you? Do recurrences draw you back in time? Are you nostalgic for lost futures? Does the present seem ghostly? Is it already absent? Are your ghosts tied to habits, places, memories, acts? What haunts you as a writer? What haunts, real or metaphorical, have you visited and revisited? Do your hauntings make you smile? Do they obsess you?

LAURA ESQUIVEL | CONTACTO CON FANTASMAS

Do I have contact with ghosts? Of course I do. Where, you might ask? What type of ghosts? When, and how?

I would love to say that I can see ghosts, but that would be a lie. I do, though, confess that I constantly hear voices. Before you try to diagnose me with schizophrenia, let me explain: When I hear the voices, it's a much more subtle experience than when I talk to a friend, yet more convincing at the same time. Still, it would be deceitful to maintain that these other murmurs are more real.

It happens when I walk through the markets, when I take a stroll in the park or along the beach, when I write, and when I cook, but especially when I step in the shower and feel the flowing water on my body, face, and head. Running water always floods me with presences and words that roll over me like waterfalls of joy and revelation. Bathing or showering has always been an intense and healing experience for me. During this activity I hear ideas, texts, and dialogues that I then integrate into my writing. I can even talk to dead friends or family members outside of time. Are these voices real? I don't know, but I certainly do hear them. There are other voices that keep me company as I carry out my daily activities, but they're different than the ones the water brings.

I love to walk down market aisles. The first dialogue I establish with food is when I purchase ingredients for a recipe. It's a wonderful act of seduction. Fish, chiles, ginger, peppers, onions, basil, and cilantro all call out to me. Each ingredient begs me to smell it, to touch it, to taste it. There's nothing quite as pleasing as plunging one's hand into a sack of beans, of rice, of lentils, or of corn kernels, our sacred foodstuffs that have nourished most Mesoamerican tongues. How to deny that the spirit of corn speaks to us? One just has to be willing to listen, and the miracle happens. The choosing of ingredients to prepare a meal is undoubtedly the first nutritious dialogue that constitutes us as individual beings.

Once I am finished shopping for the day and back in my kitchen, I listen to the bubbling water that I placed on the stove as it tells me that it's ready to receive the chocolate. I listen to the fire when it suggests I turn down its flame so the food doesn't burn. I listen to the pestle of my molcajete as it rhythmically sways and crushes the chiles, onion, and to-matoes, until its sound lets me know that the salsa is ready. Of course, I also hear my mother's voice saying "Honey, take the beans off the stove," or "Add a little bit more cumin," or "The broth will be too salty now, add some potatoes to correct it." To prepare any recipe is to come into con-tact with the ghosts of our ancestors. The ghosts of seeds, stones, uten-sils, people, and animals. Within the alchemical laboratory known as the kitchen, history becomes the voice of hundreds—or maybe millions—of beings that become one in order to relive the human experience. Inside the kitchen, voices run together, becoming one collective breath of life that seeks to affirm its existence through contact with an individual be-ing who dares to interact with a past full of murmurs and souls.

But without a doubt, the greatest and most sublime experience of contact with ghosts and apparitions comes when one consumes the food. The slow savoring of a dish one has prepared is like reading a great work of literature. The other's presence is there, it can be felt, smelled, tasted, and it fills us with joy when it becomes clear that the apparition is real. That it's always possible to reestablish a real dialogue with the entire universe. That the supposed silence of the souls is a myth. That we are never alone. Ever.

JOYCE CAROL OATES | RECIPE IN DEFIANCE OF GRIEF

Something simple like scrambled eggs with onions and smoked salmon and a particular sort of sourdough bread, and he might've had a glass of wine, possibly two glasses of wine, and there'd certainly have been a salad, mostly red-leaf lettuce, though with some of those little red cherry tomatoes he grew in his garden; and thin-sliced cucumbers, and thin-sliced red peppers; for it's a household custom for him to make a simple meal when you've been traveling, and to put a small vase of flowers on your desk for you to discover when you return. And it comes as a slow revelation to you—you who are dazed with travel, both at the time and now years later recalling that time across an abyss of such depth and vertigo you dare not glance into it—that yes, this is the last meal he will prepare for the two of you, the last meal he will prepare on such an occasion, or on any occasion, on this wintry evening in February 2008, as it is the last time you will set the table for two and light the dining room candles in the glass-walled house; and so you are thinking that possibly you can't prepare the simple meal that had been one of your customs, for it's too soon, and you aren't ready; you aren't strong enough; a recipe in defiance of grief is one of those gestures thrilling in poetry but unrealizable in life. So thinking, *Maybe another evening, maybe this year, or next. Or maybe not ever. And to whom will it matter?—almost no one. Just one.*

ELEANOR WILNER | THE LOVE OF WHAT IS NOT

Haunting? For me, it is natural order defied: What is dead or gone or absent has borrowed from the living some of our energy, and thus what haunts us is felt as a drain, parasitic, like ticks swollen with the blood of the living. I recall the scene in *The Odyssey* where the shades of the dead are brought to speech only by drinking the hot blood of a newly sacrificed animal. So what is gone becomes something lively, but that liveliness is felt as an uncanny depletion because it is drawn from our living energy. The haunt is nothing without us; it is like the blood disease, nostalgia, of the Swiss mercenary soldiers who came down to fight in the lowlands—just so, we carry this haunting within and yet fear the power we give it.

What fascinates me is the rich way that language embeds experience and history, and how a word can slowly shift from depicting habitual easiness to its opposite, a habitual uneasiness. Because, given its roots and past usages, haunting begins with dwelling, tracing back through several language layers to a distant relation to the proto-Germanic word for "home." Whether or not that etymology is partly surmise, it seems evident that the word's early use denoted a place habitually visited or dwelled in, as a woodland pond was called the haunt of dragonflies. That usage survives, but the negative use has become ascendant.

I wonder if the loss of home with the endless wars, migrations, and emigrations, so much a part of the history that English inherits, didn't bring loss (beyond that of childhood) into the heart of the sense of home, and so make of it a ghostly thing, a haunting memory that won't let go, a haunt in the later, present sense—a lost world that won't entirely depart, so its ghostly presence saps energy from the present. Nostalgia like a leaking tire, whose stale, slightly sweet escaping air slowly deflates what carries us forward, so we are haunted, stuck, drawn back toward what is gone. But I want to speak here of a special kind of haunting—that by what we only dream was home.

This imagined loss I set somewhat apart from the many other kinds, like the haunting that comes from having failed in some essential relation to someone now dead, or from the emigrant longing for a lost language and landscape, or from an experience of atrocity that recurs and recurs, and continues to drain one's vitality. With all sympathy toward those forms of haunting, I am going here to become less forgiving as I enter the province of poetry: I am going to indulge in a little Eurydice rant.

Isn't Orpheus a man haunted, no, twice haunted—once by the loss of a young "unravish'd bride of quietness" (to borrow Keats's usage), and then by her second loss as the ghost who followed him toward their unlived life? Until, of course, he famously looked back. And now I must admit how tiresome I find this cult of the never-had, the loss of what never was, like the "pro-life" adoration of the unborn, the sigh (and even ages hence!) at the road not taken—what makes all real encounters a disappointment, as they are compared with what was ideally imagined but never tested in the fires of reality. Figures like Eurydice, standing in the eerie gauze of their ghostly presence, between the man and his happiness. Between the living and their lives. And how easily we are brought to desire what we don't or can't have. And this, for one who swears by imagination as the best intelligence we've got, is damned upsetting.

And, by the way, I do not for a moment mean this as another American mouthing the psychobabble of "move on," "turn the page," when faced with real loss. For grief is not that kind of thing at all; it is not yearning after what never happened, what never was, nor after the lost, unconscious grace of an idealized infancy. (Freud, too, it seems to me, was a poet of nostalgia, haunted by an idyllic state he imagined.) Always with haunting is the unresolved, the undone, the not-yet-born, the un-lived, the only imaginary. I have been talking about the love of what is not, not the love of what is, or the love of what most certainly was.

And Eurydice? Perhaps her disappearance when he looked back was the apprehension of the real woman, for she was that on her own terms—a knowledge that he would always be looking back to the lost Eurydice, and how could she ever compete with her own ghost?

WILLIE PERDOMO | ANOTHER KIND OF OPEN

Call me Beatrice. Call me Laura. No. Call me *negra, dark goddess.* Call me Juana O.

Like Juana Bayona, Juana la Loca, or Juana Peña. No. More like Juana O Shit, Juana O Wow, Juana O Baby, Juana O Damn, Juana O My Darling—Juana O, only for you, your singular love, your bad bitch, your siempre, your jones, your final image on a rainy day, the street that wears your name.

Here I am, in the middle of a lunch poem, and I'm fast on a shade of brown, butter going soft, an autumn leaf stuck to a boot heel when I think of you.

You wrote poems for me like I was never there.

Not here, you would say…

When we met, you swore I was your primary source. Years later, I see you're still taking bows & working for claps. My mother used to say, *If he learns to talk, take his good measure, check his spelling, see if he slaps his books on the table when he makes them.*

After all the games had been played, you still wanted to take a bite out of me.

Everyone wants the moments, but where's the soft word for leaving?

What was wild about you was wild about me. Let the noble heart respond, boo. Your poems lacked peonies, ponies, and suffering. Go copy some crazy tap kisses.

My measurement beyond meter? How much light you block. Why me, why me that's always telling you my dreams?

Go ahead. Test me. I ain't no poet, but I can see.

KIMIKO HAHN | SAFE DEPOSIT BOX #321
THAT I HAVEN'T OPENED IN TWO YEARS

Mother's Tibetan necklace, an upside-down donkey with its legs "tied" to the bail ring. Small coral and turquoise beads, three on each side of the pendant.

Black tsuba that Mother wore as a pendant. Dad's Navy I.D. bracelet. A teething ring—but what infant could bite down on a mother-of-pearl ring and silver bell, even with her little gums—?

Great-Grandpa Leonhardt's Twenty-Five Years' Employment diamond pin from the Harley-Davidson Factory—where he was an inventor. Milwaukee.

EE bonds that Ted and I saved for the girls' education, bought with money inherited from his mother and from my NEA grant. One of the six cashed.

Wedding rings: one from my first marriage to Shigemi, and one from my marriage to Ted—I wonder if he has kept his. Or where he has, if not here. But I can't ask.

Mother's passport photo, 1955. (Is she holding me?)

Flash drive with evidence of his infidelity.

[Until I open the box to cash another bond, I will not know that Mother's spiky coral necklace that I thought Tomie inherited, and that I coveted but didn't want to admit, is actually in here. Mine all along.]

lack of community. Everyone is haunted.

There is a new study with a drug that can make you forget particular memories. Traumatic experiences leave a dense trail. They etch the DNA with chemical marks in the genome. These memories can gather and produce the condition of PTSD. Now there is a class of drugs called histone deacetylase inhibitors (HDACs) which clear epigenetic marks from DNA if used with therapy that recreates the fear conditioning. But how would we get a whole cavalry into a therapist's room? And how to simulate massacre?

We are all riding PTSD horses in this country, fleeing from the Puritans, from the stories of violence that allowed this country to be imagined into an experimental democracy of mostly decent people, who are all still haunted.

And now the evidence that black holes are making gravitational waves and we will be able to see all the way back to the creation of the world, if it is still there after the wave crests. I wonder if the scientists considered the undertow of warped space around the black holes? The collision makes a sound larger than any other sound in the universe. I will be haunted thinking of the immensity of this sound, and how it shifts DNA to allow this memory of the discovery in our consciousness. Scientists know this by math poetry. But can they hear the singing?

ALICIA OSTRIKER | PRACTICE

I am practicing my music. We are a triangle: myself, my laptop—thanks to which I can access MP3 versions of my alto parts online—and Joseph Haydn, incarnated (or reincarnated) in the form of the sheet music of his *Heiligmesse.*

We don't usually think of it that way. I mean, is the actual person present in the works of art he or she leaves behind?

Yes, why not? Isn't that the best kind of afterlife? At any rate, I have been struggling to learn my part in the Mass. It is difficult for me because I never learned to read music; my family could not afford to give me music lessons. But I sang an enthusiastic soprano in high school and college. In college we did Beethoven's 9th with the Boston Symphony Orchestra and the Boston University Symphonic Chorus. I rose to high C when Schiller and Beethoven's dream of human brotherhood took us there, and sailed along as on a gust of wind. When I was twenty, if I heard a melody I could reproduce it. But my soprano voice is gone and alto parts are harder and I can't pick it up the way I could and I still can't read music.

I joined this chorus, the Collegiate Singers, two years ago. We do wonderful work, but I struggle. Slowly, slowly, I am learning. It is becoming easier. Now each semester, there comes a moment when I pull my boots out of the mud, climb into the boat, and sail. The sky over my head a clean blue with some fluffy clouds. It's as if I have been beating a long while at the locked doors of a castle, which finally open, and I walk in.

As this happens, as I enter the music, the feelings the Mass exists to express enter my mind and heart. Mind and heart together, as they should be; in Hebrew one word, "lev," means both. It's a strong piece, and at some moment it struck me that Haydn believed the familiar words of the Mass that he was setting, and was creating music that would technically carry the meaning of those words, the emotion of them. Carry the meaning as a parent might hold a beautiful and tender newborn. Lord, have mercy on us. Glory to God in the highest. I believe. Holy holy holy. Blessed be. Lamb of God. There's profound personal longing, there's excited awe, there's confidence, there's pain, there's the reassurance of imagining ourselves sitting next to our father's right hand, safe and loved.

It seems to make no difference that I am not a Christian and don't in fact believe the words I am singing. Don't "believe" in the God I am so ardently addressing. It seems the feelings that belong to these words arise from somewhere within myself and are sent sailing out and might sail to the uttermost perimeters of the universe, where God collects and recycles them.

By "God," I mean whatever you think is the ultimate shaping force in the universe, or whatever you think is sacred or divine. It might not be anything defined by churches or synagogues or mosques. But the churches have done a great job creating language, creating music, that expresses our yearning to be loved by that force. Our yearning to praise it.

It's the same with poetry. The words are one thing and the emotion is another; they are connected by music. From time to time, we encounter words that lead us through the door. We are (briefly) saved. We find ourselves in a landscape or seascape, a landscape or seascape of the soul. "There is another world, but it is inside this one," Paul Éluard is supposed to have said. Sometimes, for minutes at a time, we can be there.

Modernism mostly swept the sacred away. But it lingers on, in our determinedly secular and cynical era, and not only in the churches, synagogues, and mosques, but—more importantly, perhaps more authentically—in the imagination of the artists. It never disappears entirely, but right now it is leading a kind of underground life in today's poetry. It's below the radar of the critics. The same with visual art and music, yes? The life of the spirit surges on, regardless. Amen.

AMITAVA KUMAR | THE BOY IN THE WARD

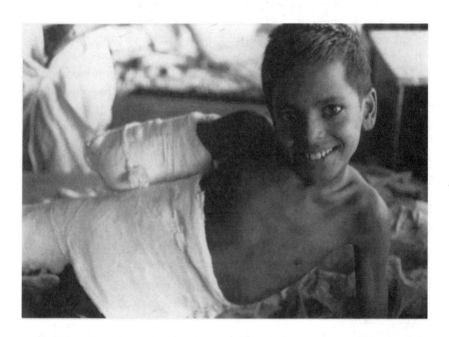

My elder sister was working as a doctor in a hospital in the small town of Darbhanga, in Bihar, in the mid-1990s. I met this boy there. He had fallen from a tree and broken his hip, and also his arm and leg. His parents sat beside him. Some days back, they had brought him to the hospital from their village, but it was already too late. The doctors had to amputate the boy's right arm because the gangrene had begun to spread.

I think of that boy sometimes. What became of him? I was still young when I took this picture. I didn't have a family. I have two children now. That boy I met in the hospital's general ward must now be a grown man. Does he, too, have a family now? I'm certain that despite his disability he is enormously skilled at what he does, perhaps farming or herding animals in a village in Bihar. One day the thought came that he could be driving a three-wheeled scooter, an auto-rickshaw, that are used to ferry passengers on the crowded Indian streets. I actually saw a disabled man driving an auto-rickshaw in Delhi and I recalled the boy from two decades ago.

For the most part, I'm haunted by his smile.

ELENA PONIATOWSKA | THE VOICES OF OTHERS

Who or what haunts you?
As I am to be eighty-four in May and am a Mexican, my dead ones haunt me, especially my mother because I always feel I didn't care for her enough or spend enough time with her. My only brother, Jan Poniatowski, died at twenty-one and I felt I should live for him instead of living with her.

Do recurrences draw you back in time?
Of course the disappearance of forty-three students in Ayotzinapa reminds me of the killing of the students in Mexico in 1968. I wrote *Massacre in Mexico* for them and I am now writing prologues and more prologues for books currently being published about this new Mexican massacre.

Are you nostalgic for lost futures?
Mexico is a country that eats you up. I remember speaking at the Cervantes Institute to the extraordinary Siri Hustvedt, who in Manhattan centers her life on her work. I loved her books and felt envious because she does with them what she wants and writes about what she wants. This has not happened to me. Mexico invades you, Mexico makes it impossible to think about anything other than Mexico, and there is very little chance to live for yourself and to stay away from Mexico's life, its people, its students. Life outside barges in and takes over. Whatever you are doing seems stupid and useless next to what is happening: murder, disappearances, torture, an army accused of drug-trafficking and a president's useless rhetoric in a White House purchased the first year of his term that has scandalized all Mexicans. Corruption is equal to the government itself. To be naïve in politics is to be very dumb and I have been naïve and dumb, which is the worst way to live in Mexico today.

Does the present seem ghostly? Is it already absent?
The present is very real as is old age, although old age makes me happy.

There are so many privileges in my life today. People acknowledge me and are more than supportive. I feel that young university students take care of me as do my ten grandchildren. Even when it is not needed, people offer me their arm. There are always flowers and trees coming through my window. Happiness makes me wake up with a smile and I live very happily in spite of the tragedy of my country. It is not because I am a selfish person; it is just because I have a happy nature inherited from my mother who, even after the death of her only son, knew how to smile to others and listen to their stories, as boring as they might be, even those of old Mexicans who were always going on about their aches, pains, and misfortunes.

Are your ghosts tied to habits, places, memories, acts? What haunts you as a writer?

As a writer, I miss not having written about myself because I have been haunted by the voices of others ever since 1953, when I became a journalist. Journalism is like a drug; it is very difficult to get it out of your system. But it is also very humbling because it makes you wait for others and listen to others. It is a great lesson in humility, and I have had many.

What haunts, real or metaphorical, have you visited and revisited? Do your hauntings make you smile? Do they obsess you?

At nearly 84, what obsesses me is leaving my children behind because they depend on me more than American boys and girls depend on their parents. The same happens to my ten grandchildren, and the last one is only nine. But I feel like the grandmother of all Mexican children who sleep in the streets and wash windshields at stoplights and eat standing up on street corners. There are no schools for them and they have no future. The Mexican politicians couldn't care less and the national budget does nothing for education. There is hunger, but schools are also indispensable and many extraordinarily talented boys and girls are doomed to death as was the little Syrian child photographed dead on a beach in Turkey.

What are your habits?

I have very few habits, which is a blessing. Once my American grandmother, Elizabeth Sperry Crocker, who went from California to Paris to marry Prince André Poniatowski, told me that it was easy to enslave yourself, even to a pair of slippers, and that there were many who couldn't even get up if they couldn't find theirs. This advice has accompanied me all my life and has made my feet free from bindings, which makes me similar to a huge number of barefoot Mexicans. It also makes me similar to dogs, cats, birds, parrots, horses who even fly without shoes.

SANTA RITA DE LOS IMPOSIBLES

Adriana E. Ramírez

JULY 1, 2007—He chose to die in American pants. "No, no no. What he thought were American pants," my mother corrected me. The Italian brand had a factory in Medellín, but common folk swore they were American.

"No, no," my mother continued her correction. "Pablo Angel died in Colombian blue jeans." She said this in English so that my grandma wouldn't know I saw the dead boy on the street.

"But," I whispered back to Mom, "he wanted to die in American pants, he chose what to him was an American brand, he wanted to die in Diesel jeans."

"I don't think that he thought about it. Guys don't think. Guys do the strangest things, it's what makes us all guys."

She meant people, as in *People don't think.* My mother calls all groups of people "guys."

She continued, "Guys don't think, 'Oh, I'll wear a nice dress or pants' when they are going to die. They think, 'Oh, shit! I'm going to die!'"

"But he knew, he knew he was going to die today. He must have thought about it. Maybe they were his favorite jeans."

"They were expensive jeans for him," my mother countered.

"Maybe. I wonder if he knew how he was going to die."

"Ay, tú, there aren't too many places to be shot: the head, the heart, the arm, the leg. You think he was trying to match pants to blood?"

"I would have worn a white shirt too. The contrast was beautiful."

My grandmother interrupted, clearing her throat. She was tired of our English conversation. "I will probably die in American jeans—my brother did."

Adriana E. Ramírez won the 2015 PEN Fusion/Emerging Writers Prize for her manuscript *Dead Boys*.

Pablo Angel chose to die in what he thought were American pants. I believe this. He left the house early in the morning. He bought a card to recharge his cellphone. He knew he was going to die; he only bought twenty-five minutes. Made his last phone call and waited. The news said he owed too much money. Had borrowed it all to buy out his government-required military service.

You can buy your way out of the draft here, a few phone calls if you dance at the right parties or you're willing to borrow enough—thousands in a country where few make hundreds. Pablo Angel preferred the loan shark to the guerrilla. A year's worth of interest added up faster than he could pay. He'd been warned. Several times. And then one day he woke up, put on his Diesel jeans (manufactured in Medellín) with a white shirt. He'd been told, his mother said, that it would be before noon.

Like a good Catholic, Pablo Angel went to church. He knelt with his back to the road out of Barranquilla and prayed for an hour to a God that understood the value of dying in nice pants, a God that understood the goodness in his choices. The highway to Medellín and out of Barranquilla begins at the old church, Santa Rita, patron saint of all the miracles that never come.

I sat in the passenger side of my aunt Martha's car and watched the crowd gathering beside us as we inched our way through traffic. I saw his body for three minutes. One hundred and eighty seconds that Martha and I didn't speak, both staring at the body, formerly a boy.

The cumbia music on the radio stopped. A woman began talking about North American celebrities in Cartagena. The word DIESEL was written below the pocket of Pablo Angel's pants. The blood poured dry out of a hole near his stomach. Mel Gibson's plane had touched down in Colombia, according to the woman on the radio. The boy was dead, no one tried to help him. Everyone just stood and watched as the policeman approached with cloth to cover Pablo Angel's head. President Bush's visit earlier in the year alerted Colombian officials to national security problems; the news break's theme music played once again.

The dead face before me was frozen somewhere between surprise and laughter. Pablo Angel left a stain on the sidewalk, his blood trying to make a record before being cleaned off. But he did right in picking that white shirt. Crimson-soaked, the body had surrendered, its flag coolly kissing the cobblestone.

A policeman waved us on. *How odd*, my aunt would say to me, *that it was during the day, so public. Seemed amateurish. Like a cheap circus.*

I called my mother on the cellphone. I explained that I'd seen a dead boy in a white shirt on the gray stones of a courtyard. A minute into the conversation the call dropped—the line dead.

We stopped two blocks later and bought precious minutes from a street vendor. "Minutos de Comcel por ochenta y cinco pesos el minuto." I did the math in my head. Five cents for a minute. I considered how many I would need for the remainder of my time in Colombia. I bought two hundred.

Better, the dead boy's mother said through tears in broken Spanish on the news that night, *than dying in the jungle against the guerrilla, the government, the parapacos, or any of the other delusional souls that keep us honest.*

"Mejor?" My grandmother did not pity the woman on the television. "Pendeja."

This woman was an idiot. My grandmother had lost a sister and a brother. My mother had lost her father and her son. I've lost them, too. We knew that being shot down by a loan shark was not a blessing.

"Pendeja."

"Sí. Es una pendeja." Three generations of women in my family agreed. Once my grandmother started saying things like "pendeja," we were all allowed to jump in. My mother and I never missed an opportunity for sanctioned cursing.

LONELY WOMEN

Seungja Choi
Translated by Cathy Park Hong and Won-Chung Kim

Lonely women
wait for the phones to ring, which never ring.
Lonelier women are petrified
when their phones—that have never rung—suddenly ring.
Much lonelier women are afraid
that their phones—that have never rung—may suddenly ring,
and their hearts may stop.
Still, much lonelier women pretend to be asleep
or actually sleep when all the world's lovers
call them at once.

long time to pluck up the courage to talk to other Muslim women about this stuff because of the guilt. I'm so open about it in my book because I hope younger Muslim women reading this book share, either with me or with their friends, their journey to their own sexuality, in whichever direction and form it takes. So I mention those things, although I know that they're going to be difficult for my family to read. Where I come from, it's not common for women to talk about sex, and that's exactly why I did it: because these are revolutionary times.

"We're going through a global feminist moment."

When eighteen female revolutionaries were sexually assaulted under the guise of so-called virginity testing after the Tahrir Square protests in Egypt, there was more anger directed toward us, the women who exposed this horrendous crime, than toward the military that assaulted us. All the outrage that should have been directed at the men who were trying to break us, and sexually assaulting us, and dragging us through the streets, was being directed toward the women—and not toward the trifecta of patriarchies I call the State, the Street, and the Home.

But I believe we're going through a global feminist moment. In China, just after International Women's Day, at least ten feminists were arrested for protesting against misogyny and patriarchy, and five of them are still in jail. We saw women in India rise up after the Delhi gang rape; they've been speaking out against sexual violence for a long time, but we finally got to hear their voices. We saw women in Afghanistan who insisted on burying the woman called Farkhunda after her lynching, and they broke with Muslim tradition to do that. We saw women in Turkey who did the same after a woman was raped and killed, and they told the local imam, "No, we will not abide by your tradition. No other man will touch her, and we will bury her." And here in this country, we saw three queer black women launch Black Lives Matter after Trayvon Martin was murdered.

The common thread is we are all women of color. In my part of the world, we're often told feminism is a Western import, it's not part of our culture or religion. But all of these women are saying, "We're tired of having to choose between racism and sexism," and having to fight Islamophobia and xenophobia in parts of the world where Muslims live as minorities, having to fight against that and having to fight against misogyny. More and more women are saying, "It is our right and it is our role to criticize the misogyny from within and without, and also fight those who are attacking Islam."

"There is no country that has gotten rid of misogyny."

When people in the U.S. say, "Muslim men are this, Muslim men are that," I bring in the Christian Brotherhood, and talk about what the right wing in this country has done to women's reproductive rights, the abortion clinics that have had to close in the South, the case of Purvi Patel in Indiana, who's gone to jail on charges of feticide—and you've hardly heard a thing, because she is a disempowered, brown, Hindu woman. When that starts to happen to white Christian women, then maybe we will hear a big fuss.

During my thirteen years in the U.S., especially in the South and at the University of Oklahoma, I'd often describe those regions as the Middle East, because there were so many similarities between the two: the conservatives, the religion, and the patriarchy. In the Middle East we fight the Muslim Brotherhood; here in the U.S. we fight the Christian Brotherhood. Men of the extreme right of any religion are obsessed with our vaginas, and my message to them is, "Stay out of my vagina unless I want you in there."

That's a really important thing to remember, because the religious right has whittled us away through sexuality and the control of our bodies. There's a connection between "modesty culture," where you wear a hijab or a niqab and you cover your face, and "purity culture," where you sign a virginity pledge to your father until you get married, where your community is obsessed with your purity and your body.

When people say misogyny in the Middle East is caused by colonization, I say, "Yes, we had colonial history, and it was awful, but we got rid of the Brits in Egypt over fifty years ago." What have we done since then to reverse the misogyny? What have all these countries done since they liberated themselves from occupation and colonial powers?

It's not about political engagement, it's not about poverty, it's not about wealth, it's not about how long ago we got rid of colonization—it's about misogyny and patriarchy. There is no country that has gotten rid of misogyny. Those of you who follow global politics will remember when the Swedish foreign minister tried to take a stand on feminist principles against Saudi Arabia, and the Arab League prevented her from speaking because the Saudis were able to dominate the Arab League. She tried to make a point about a blogger who was supposed to receive a thousand lashes (he was only flogged once because of international outcry), but she was also going to make a point about Saudi Arabia's horrendous women's rights record. She was attacked in Sweden by the business community—this is Sweden, and yet this woman was called "emotional." She was also told that she didn't have a grasp of international diplomacy. This is the Swedish foreign minister! Clearly, misogyny is global.

"Fight your fight here."

What you can do to help me, and the women in the region from where I come and about which I write, is to fight your fight here. At least 25 percent of women on college campuses in this country experience a form of sexual assault. Fight that. Fight against what the religious right wing is doing to women's reproductive rights in this country. Because believe me, the men that I am fighting where I come from read these statistics and say, "Do you know how many women are raped every five minutes in America?" as if that makes anything better. But they just shrug, and they say, "You see, even in America, that country that you keep talking about, where you lived, they still treat women badly." So fight your fight here, and fight, most importantly, complacency. I think complacency is so dangerous. So many young women will just shrug and say, "I don't need to be a feminist, everything's been solved." No, we are post-nothing. If anything, the past few in this country have taught us that we're not post-racism, we're not post-sexism, we are post-nothing.

Hold your political representatives to account for the hypocrisy that allows them to throw women like cheap bargaining chips across the table when they meet with Middle Eastern regimes. If they dare bring up the issue of women and misogyny, and then these regimes say, "It's none of your business, it's our religion," respond with, "Women's rights are human rights, and it is our business." The State Department produces a Human Rights Report every year, with a section in every report on women's rights, and they know what it's like. They know that in the year 2002, fifteen schoolgirls were burned to death in Saudi Arabia because they weren't veiled. What kind of culture allows a morality police, basically a militia made up of zealots, to choose a veil over a girl's life?

There should have been a revolution in Saudi Arabia when those girls died, and absolutely nothing happened. When the U.S. secretary of state goes to a country like that and says nothing, it is a crime. When John Kerry goes to Saudi Arabia after women have engaged in acts of nonviolent civil disobedience against the ban on driving, and he's asked, "What do you think of what the women did?" and he essentially says, "The social environment in Saudi Arabia is none of our business," that is the equivalent of someone going to South Africa during apartheid and shrugging—because what is happening in Saudi Arabia is gender apartheid, and we have to name it as such.

"The revolution really is personal."

After Tahrir Square, when they broke my arms and sexually assaulted me, I was not only robbed of the ability to write for three months because my arms were in casts, but I felt that I lost a great sense of beauty. Soon after I was attacked, Gloria Steinem sent me a kind email and suggested I read a wonderful book called *Trauma and Recovery*, by the feminist psychiatrist Judith Herman. In this book, Judith Herman connects sexual violence and the ensuing trauma with the PTSD that war veterans experience. She makes a wonderful point about how war veterans have things like the Tomb of the Unknown Soldier, and recognition from society that they performed an honorable role. Whereas those of us who survive sexual violence often feel that we've lost something. I feel that I lost a great sense of beauty, but there is nowhere we can go to honor that. There is no monument to the unknown sister.

I remember becoming a feminist at the age of nineteen and feeling fucking terrified. I knew that I was opening a door and walking down a corridor I could never turn back on. You understand that this choice is going to destroy the patriarchy, of course, but by destroying everything that you've been taught—everything your family has taught you, everything your religion has taught you. So I try to imagine nineteen-year-old me, and how scared I was: *Headscarves and Hymens* is for her. I get so many tweets, and all these people write me the most ridiculous things like, "The Middle East is falling apart, why are you talking about sex?" As if sex is not an important thing. My answer to them is that sex is about consent and agency, and what is a revolution without consent and agency? Then I get asked, "Well, women in the Middle East are struggling with literacy and employment and—" What? Because you're poor, you shouldn't have consent and agency, and the right to enjoy your body, and the right to enjoy sex with whomever you want? Because you can't read or write, your body is not yours and doesn't belong to you? So sex is central to this, sex is something I spent many years of my life struggling around and against, and that guilt, why? Every time I hold readings like this, I hear from Muslim women who share their stories because they need someone to speak first. It took me the longest time to be able to share sex and guilt with fellow Muslim and Arabic women; why can we not even speak to each other about this? Consent and agency and sex are integral to our liberation, and that's why I insist on speaking about these things.

EBOLA

Aminatta Forna

After the fourth day the rats started to emerge in groups to die. They came up from the basements and cubby-holes, cellars and drains, in long swaying lines; they staggered in the light, collapsed and died, right next to people. At night, in corridors and side-streets, one could clearly hear the tiny squeaks as they expired. In the morning, on the outskirts of town, you would find them stretched out in the gutter with a little floret of blood on their pointed muzzles, some blown up and rotting, others stiff, with their whiskers still standing up.

—*The Plague*, by Albert Camus

September 6, 2014
A series of texts from my cousin Morlai in Sierra Leone:

Ebola is spreading like wildfire in Harmattan.
The situation is grave.
Families are wiped out.
Even elderly people raid us for food.
What the government is saying is not what is happening.
People are abandoned to die in hospital.
Doctors are dying.
People are quarantined without food.
We are in trouble.
We are dying like rats.

Rats spread Ebola. Bats. Flying rats. They nested in the rafters of houses and their contaminated piss and shit dropped onto the floors and the furniture of the people below. By tending to the sick, the humans contaminated each other through acts of love. The virus killed the mothers and the wives. It killed the traditional healers. It killed the nurses and the doctors. It killed the world's leading expert on hemorrhagic fevers,

This transcript is adapted from remarks made at the 2015 PEN World Voices Festival.

and it killed everybody who worked for him in his research institute.

On Facebook, someone posts a photograph of a corpse lying in the street outside his house. Blood bubbles from the man's mouth. A bright red "floret of blood." The modern and the medieval collide. We communicate with our quarantined families by text. My mother lets all but one of the servants go. In the village they sequester themselves and turn away strangers. The harvest ripens and then withers. No traveling teams of laborers arrive to help gather the rice. When a person dies, strange angels in white suits appear. At first the people tried to chase them away; now they watch while the angels perform their rituals, cleansing the house and the corpse with chlorine. The angels stand in a line and bow to the deceased before they bear them away to a mass grave. On the internet each week someone posts a roster of the dead, no names, just numbers. And every week still I scan them to see how many dead in our locality.

In Sierra Leone we are used to being looked at without pity. For a long time help did not come. Then the rich countries sent money, but it was too late. Here now was something new, a problem you couldn't buy your way out of. We needed doctors and nurses, but the rich countries didn't want to send theirs. Instead, doctors, nurses, and logisticians of the diaspora took leave from their jobs and became reverse refugees, headed toward the danger.

One day in September, I reach Morlai on the telephone. He is moving his children to the village from the city, where the danger is worst. He is curious to understand why help is so long in coming. I tell him people are tired of Africa and its problems. He says: "This is not a problem of Africa's making."

I tell him the Islamic State is beheading American and British men and posting the videos on the internet. That's all the newspapers report, all anybody is talking about.

"So we must wait for a white person to catch ebola?" he asks.

"Yes," I say. I can hear him breathe.

Finally he says: "Then we must only be patient."

PRAYER BEFORE DYING

Edwidge Danticat

I grew up in houses where we prayed every morning and every night. First with my minister uncle in Haiti. Then with my parents and brothers in Brooklyn. Yet it was very hard for me to write a prayer for this evening. I think this is in part because I was taught that our prayers are meant to be private.

The prayers of the people in my life usually highlighted our most urgent desires. There were times when we prayed for food. Times when we prayed for loved ones to be released from jail. Times later on when we would pray for our family members, including our parents, not to die.

Still, our most profound prayers are prayers of gratitude. Or so my mother used to say. Simply saying mèsi or thank you is in itself a prayer. Saying souple, s'il vous plait, please, can also be a kind of prayer.

When my mother was dying of cancer, she and I prayed together a lot. The Bible says to "pray without ceasing," she kept reminding me.

I remember the exact moment when she stopped praying to be healed and started praying for peace, la pè, her shorthand for a peaceful transition. We called those final prayers our surrender prayers.

I used to tell myself that writing is a kind of prayer, that silence can be prayer, that even children are prayers, living and growing prayers. That love is the most powerful prayer of all.

My prayer is inspired by my mother. It is the prayer I imagined her saying in her head during her final moments on this Earth, during those final minutes when she couldn't speak anymore but could still hear a little bit, as she was drifting away.

These remarks are adapted from the "Prayers and Meditations" event at the 2015 PEN World Voices Festival

Dear Lord,

Please let this be my final prayer, my very final prayer. Let there be no more need for me to ask anything else of you and of this sometimes shaken and sometimes troubled but beautiful Earth. Please let this be the last time I think of you, before we see each other face-to-face, light-to-light, wind-to-wind, sky-to-sky, or however we will be.

I can't wait. I can't wait to see what I will be: what colors, what shade, what light pillar, what rainbow, what moonbow, what sunbow, what glory, or what new sky.

Please let me now accept all of this. As I have already accepted this world and all that it is and has been.

And please let the world go on. Let the sun still rise and set. Let the rain still fall, quiet and soft at times, and hard at other times. Let the oceans be still or roar, as they always have. Please let the world go on as it always has, so that my children will know that only my spark has dimmed and not the entire world.

Please let my children remember me. Both the good and bad of me. Let them not forget one thing about me that could help them be better women and men.

Please let the pain racking my body stop. Let it stop right now. Please let my lungs stop aching. Please let my breath stop sounding like hammers in my ear. Please don't let all these drugs make me say anything hateful at this final hour. Please make my daughter stop crying. Please let it be a sunny day when they bury me. Please let my children find the five hundred dollars I left in the tin can in the freezer—I really should have told them about that when I still could. Please don't let them throw out my good blender. All it needs is a new blade.

Okay, maybe you can make my children forget all the times I spanked them. There might not be much to be gained from that. Please let them say nice things about me at my funeral. Things

Watching you now, my face stings as it stung when my blind great-uncle
brushed my cheekbones, searching for his own face. When you died,
Tato, I took a razor to the movie looping in my head, cutting the scenes
where you curled an arm around my shoulder, all the times you would
squeeze the silence out of me so I could hear the cries and songs again.
When you died, I heard only the silences between us, the shouts belling
the air before the phone went dead, all the words melting like ice in a cup.
That way I could set my jaw and take my mother's hand at the mortuary,
greet the elders in my suit and tie at the memorial, say all the right words.

Yet my face stings at last. I rewind and watch your arm drape across
my shoulder, over and over. A year ago, you pressed a Kodak slide
of my grandfather into my hand and said: *Next time, stay longer.*
Now, in the silence that is never silent, I push the chair away
from the table and say to you: *Sit down. Tell me everything. Haunt me.*

TURNT

Juliana Spahr

Sometimes it feels like it is over and it's not.
Sometimes it feels like it has just begun and it's over.

It's dark often at these times.
Urban though, so a certain version of light too.
It's hard to predict if it will start on time or how late.
I'm often a little late and it has started. Last night, I could tell from the copters overhead that I was late.
As I walked up, the blocks around it were emptying out.
Parents pulled their children home.
The night herons settled into trees.
That's the outer ring.
As I got closer, all that was left were the blinking lights of the motorcycles blocking the intersections and the men and few women in uniforms that mill about the corner, helmets in their hands. They talked among themselves. Ignored me mainly. One told me how to get around. I did not clarify that I was walking towards.
You can hear it sometimes. It often has a soundtrack. Sometimes it has drums and brass. Sometimes just joy.
When I am late I am trying to guess its path. Last night, several times I got close to it only to be turned back by a line of cops.
They let the media through but turned me back.

Then it turned the corner and there it was.

At that moment, I melted my body into it and it embraced me.

Rosy fingered dusk and all that.

Come here, it sang, listen.

And then I was borne along by the waves all night and the whirlpool, the fig tree, and I was the bat, hanging on patiently.

Aarav came up and hugged me.

Someone grabbed me from behind and I thought it is Artem but later realized it was Berat. So much mask.

I grabbed Charlotte's hand and held it for a while when things felt dicey.

It felt dicey as they cornered us from two sides and we went down the tight side street, up the hill. Charlotte's hand.

It's like that.

Moving from isolation to the depths of friends.

At first we didn't mask up. We were poets.

Then slowly one by one we did.

As we got turnt.

As I got turnt, I mean.

Sometimes I still don't mask up. It often feels hubristic.

I keep a bandana in my pocket.

It isn't super effective. It falls down a lot.

Last night, I tied it around my neck as we walked up the side street hill. I pulled it over my face as I walked past the line of cops. I noticed Emma there, throwing eggs. I ducked. Two balloons filled with paint flew by.

Visors suddenly yellow.

She said to me, how is your heart?

And I at first worried her question.

Then I realized she meant my heart and how it was turnt.

It is good, I said, I am opening it; I am expanding it.

And I meant it.

I love you I texted Felix.

Lub u!!!!! I texted Haruto.

Texting Isabella and Jackson, I love you guys.

I miss you.

I texted love you some forty-three times in the last few years.

I texted <3 some thirty-three times.

Lub u, eighteen times.

Miss you, thirty-eight.

She said, your feed is all riots, plants, picnics, and poets.

It was an accusation.

She was noticing that I had got turnt.

And I said, my son, my son is in my feed too.

I didn't bother to argue the riot with her.

Still, oh that moment.

This poem is true. I have texted I love you and its variations over and over.

Sometimes I barely knew you.

But the names are not true.

This is not a coterie poem.

Is it a milieu poem?

Can it be a movement poem?

I took all the names of this poem and never wrote them in.

There is no electronic record of them.

I found a list of the most popular baby names for various countries in 2015, the year in which I am writing this poem. I made a list, one male and one female from each list. Then I alphabetized it. And I put these names in this poem one by one. I got to O.

But Olivia, Saanvi, Santiago, Seoyeon, Sofia, Yui, and Zeynep, I love you too.

SECRET SOURCES

WHISTLEBLOWERS, NATIONAL SECURITY, AND FREE EXPRESSION

In November, PEN America released a report that examines the scant protections for whistleblowers working in United States intelligence organizations. To mark its publication, we hosted a forum at the Newseum in Washington, D.C. Executive director of PEN America, Suzanne Nossel, interviewed former U.S. government contractor Edward Snowden via Skype. Whistleblowers Thomas Drake, former senior executive at the NSA, Jesselyn Radack of WHISPeR, the Whistleblower & Source Protection Program of ExposeFacts, and *New York Times* reporter James Risen shared their stories.

Katy Glenn Bass, deputy director of PEN America's Free Expression Program, introduced the event:

> PEN's report shows that the gaps in existing protections for intelligence community whistleblowers, the government's failure to adequately address retaliation against them, and the Obama Administration's aggressive prosecution of leakers under the Espionage Act, are damaging to freedom of expression, press freedom, and access to information in the United States. The combined impact of these elements has created a chilling effect on free expression, and affects both the willingness of government workers to expose wrongdoing and the ability of journalists to cover their revelations. This poses serious risks for the free flow of information and informed public debate that is necessary for a healthy democratic society.

The following transcripts are adapted from the evening's conversations.

"People say I live in Russia, but that's actually a misunderstanding. I live on the internet."

Edward Snowden with Suzanne Nossel

SUZANNE NOSSEL: While Americans treasure the idea of free speech and lionize individuals who stand up to authority, there is a deep skittishness when it comes to whistleblowers. They make people nervous. Why do you think that is?

EDWARD SNOWDEN: I don't think it's a huge mystery, given that the government and the press in our country have extremely tight relations. A lot of media will print allegations rather than facts, whereas whistleblowers are required to present evidence on behalf of our claims. Whenever wrongdoing is revealed—whether it's warrantless wiretapping in the Bush Administration, lies in the Vietnam War, or the lead-up to Iraq and the way intelligence was doctored—when it's an unofficial leak, we immediately get a cohort of authorized leakers saying, "This is harmful, this is dangerous, it's going to cost lives, it's going to reduce the level of safety in our society." No one ever challenges them to show facts; they become persuasive simply because we say, "These are people in positions of authority; these are serious people. If the media is giving them this level of deference, perhaps we should as well."

But they don't want to talk about the concrete harms of bad policy. They don't want to declassify a particular program; they don't want us to know what's going on. As soon as anybody has to justify their position in terms of our current modern political culture, they're losing. I think that's really why, by proxy, the public is uncomfortable. Politicians become uncomfortable anytime they have to justify why they're doing what they're doing.

When you look at this as an engineer, which is sort of natural to me, you think about it in terms of game theory. What is the optimal strategy for your side, for your tribe, whatever that is? If you're a newspaper, if you've got to scoop things to survive, and the opposition has a big story but you don't, you look for your angle. Traditionally there would be follow-on reporting, other journalists would chase new leads, but this has become difficult in the national security context. Nobody wants to talk to journalists anymore, they realize it's the kiss of death for their career and could expose them to legal charges, and so journalists naturally and understandably go, "Well, what can we report on? Well, we can go after the whistleblower. Who could it be? What does the document imply about them? What could their motivations be?"

Even if journalists get the Pulitzer Prize-winning story showing that officials broke the law, they're going to lose access as a result. Bridges will be burned within the administration, or officials will start feeding stories to competitors. It's traditional in our society for the press to become adversarial to the government in a contest for public information, but unfortunately and increasingly, particularly under this administration, the government is becoming adversarial to the press. And that's quite dangerous.

NOSSEL: Do whistleblowers' motives matter? Assuming their disclosures meet the criteria of whistleblowing and advance the public interest, does that person deserve protection regardless of motive?

SNOWDEN: If they've revealed wrongdoing, that's really all that matters. If somebody works for an organized crime group, that doesn't have any bearing on what we do with the information they give and what it means to us, provided we can determine it's factually correct.

NOSSEL: We know you're not in Russia by choice, that your options were severely limited, that you've also been critical of the Russian government for human rights and freedom of expression violations. At the same time, Masha Gessen, one of our trustees at PEN America, commented during your early days in Russia, when you met with human rights groups at the Moscow airport, that the Russian propaganda machine had not gotten so much mileage out of a U.S. citizen since Angela Davis's murder trial in 1971. I think there still is a sense among some Russian dissidents that your position is unhelpful to their cause. How do you respond to that?

SNOWDEN: That's a mistake. They're trying to argue, basically, that one individual is responsible for the bad actions of another. This is the same as critics who say I caused tech companies to lose sales. We know that's not true. No one's going to be surprised if the Russian government or the Chinese government or any other irresponsible government that is against free and open and unregulated communication on the internet uses something like this to their advantage.

The fault here also lies with the U.S. government, which actively blocked my ability to leave Russia. I applied for asylum in twenty-one countries, and many of them actually seemed favorable in response—but, for example, when Ecuador seemed to be leaning toward saying, "Yes, we're going to allow him to come here," Vice President Joe Biden called the president of Ecuador directly. When the president of Bolivia, Evo Morales, made some joke about considering granting me asylum so I could leave Russia, his plane was grounded on the orders of the president of the United States. The airspace of France, Spain, Portugal, and Italy was closed (a violation of international law), and they grounded his plane.

Where is the line between prosecution and persecution? I would argue that line becomes quite bright and quite clear when you start grounding the diplomatic flights of heads of state on their equivalent of Air Force One. If that happened to the president of the United States, it would be seen as casus belli.

NOSSEL: A couple of weeks ago, there was a vote in the European Parliament against extradition for you, a new sign of support. Might that mean at some point soon you could trade your home in Russia for one in Paris?

SNOWDEN: We'll see how that goes. I do think it's pretty extraordinary to see such a wide body, the Parliament of the European Union, saying the U.S. position on this issue is mistaken. They're actually doing what I believe is a friendly action, and a proper action. There is a growing consensus that in 2013, the U.S. government could make the argument that these disclosures would be dangerous, that they could cause harm, that maybe terrorists were going to take over, that the sky was going to fall, but it's 2015 now, and the directors of the CIA, the DIA, the NSA, the FBI, and so on have testified. They've all been begged by my largest critics in Congress, "Show us any evidence, any case where anybody has come to harm as a result of these disclosures," and they never have.

NOSSEL: When people weigh up your case, one of the things they think about is your colleagues. Your colleagues had one agenda, one purpose, and you had another. It's said you had to obtain passwords or other information from them without their knowledge.

SNOWDEN: That's not true.

NOSSEL: I'm curious about your relationship with your peers and whether you think they understand what you did, what you would say to them now, or if you have spoken with them since then.

SNOWDEN: I can't comment on whether or not I've spoken with any-body. That would obviously be a profoundly negative thing for them. What I can say is that I think a number of my colleagues would under-stand and approve of the choices that I made and the results. The people at the working level at NSA are not bad guys. They aren't criminals. They aren't people trying to get over on anything, and they aren't people trying to cause harm. They are patriotic people who want to do the right thing. They recognize that they do break laws here and there, but typically they're thinking about international laws or some foreign government's laws. They like to think that they're upholding the Constitution.

Many of them didn't even know what was going on. Even people who had top secret clearance didn't know about the warrantless wiretapping program. You have increasingly restricted circles within the intelligence community, where you can't see into this silo or that silo. What was spe-cial about me was I had a special clearance called PRIVAC, which meant I could see across silos. I saw the big picture. When I connected the dots and I showed it to colleagues, they became extremely concerned.

NOSSEL: Certainly we've seen diversity of opinion on whether it was a good idea to make the disclosures you made, and I would guess some colleagues said that doing so went strongly against their grain as loyal government employees. How do you think about those people now? Do you think they've changed their minds?

SNOWDEN: I used to keep a copy of the Constitution on my desk at the NSA in Hawaii, and I would talk to my co-workers about it, particu-larly as I thought more and more about these issues, and I gave copies to some of them, and we would talk. Some people would really think about it, some people would be concerned, but there were others who said, "The Constitution is just a piece of paper. It doesn't really matter. Bottom line, we have a job to do." Particularly when we're talking about topics like extraordinary rendition. I remember one conversation quite well: A co-worker said, "Guantánamo is a giant waste of time. If we had been doing it the right way, we would have simply kicked them out of the airplane as they were crossing the Atlantic, and then we wouldn't be dealing with this problem." That guy's mind probably hasn't changed.

NOSSEL: Let's say your lawyers succeed in striking a plea deal, and you're able to come back to the United States. Fast forward five or ten years. What are you focused on, what does your life look like?

SNOWDEN: Right now I spend almost all of my time coordinating to solve really tough technical problems in terms of how we enforce the protection of our rights, the privacy of our communications, either with academics or technologists or engineers, increasingly at the Freedom of the Press Foundation. A lot of individuals in a lot of different countries think that mass surveillance is a bad idea. They don't think that bulk collection is effective or that it keeps us safe. This is a fact: It doesn't keep us safe, it doesn't save lives, it doesn't prevent terrorist attacks. For example, the telephonic metadata program under Section 215 was warrantlessly intercepting phone calls of more or less everyone in the United States for a period of more than ten years. Not only did it never stop a single terrorist attack in the United States, it didn't make a concrete difference in a single investigation.

The Boston Marathon bombings in the United States, the *Charlie Hebdo* attacks, the attacks in Sydney, the Canadian Parliament attacks—all of these attackers were known to intelligence services beforehand.

NOSSEL: I take it you'd stay with this fight, that you're saying this is, perhaps, the fight of your life. But if you were back here, would you be in Silicon Valley, developing the next generation of encryption tools? Would you be out in the streets with a bullhorn, trying to engage the public on these issues? Would you be testifying in front of Congress? Where would you situate yourself in society if you had the opportunity to come back and wage this effort from within?

SNOWDEN: I was never a very public person before 2013. A lot of computer guys are like that; they keep to themselves, they work online, they write, they design, they engineer, but they aren't so good at being out on the streets. I'm not a politician and I don't want to be, but a lot of advocacy organizations and worthy movements have asked me to participate, and so I am spending more time on that. When it comes to the question of where I would live, what would I do, would it be different, I think it wouldn't be much different than today. You know, people say I live in Russia, but that's actually a misunderstanding. I live on the internet. That's where I spend all of my time, that's where all of my work is seen, and one of the most beautiful things about the last two years is it shows that you don't have to be in some specific spot. You don't have to be in San Francisco. Even when your government is pursuing a policy of exile, you can be everywhere and anywhere. That is powerful and liberating, and I think that will be one of the most important lessons learned as a result of the disclosures of 2013. You can't shut people up the way you used to be able to.

NOSSEL: When we think about surveillance, we think about literature as maybe the most authoritative source about the harms of the surveillance state: Kafka, Huxley, Orwell. Have those books influenced you?

SNOWDEN: I think they have. Of course I've read Huxley, I've read Orwell. When we think about this—and this perhaps may not be so popular with PEN, but...

NOSSEL: Watch out.

SNOWDEN: [laughs] Literature to me is more about a writing culture than about what's bound between two covers. And there is a writing culture, a literary culture that is growing on the internet by the day. Yes, the long-form traditional novel has an influence, it has a space to make an argument that you don't get in the typical back and forth of the internet, but I think it's not helpful to give space to the idea that the internet and traditional print are in opposition to each other. I think it's an evolution as we develop new tools. Just as the printing press meant that we shared books and ideas more broadly than when each book was handwritten and an incredibly precious object, the internet is providing a reach for ideas that aren't necessarily able to attain the attention of a well-known reviewer at *The New York Times*.

AUDIENCE: By your own estimations, in what ways have you been both an effective and a less than ideal messenger for the causes of civil liberties and digital privacy?

SNOWDEN: I think the fact that I have a face is problematic. Ideally, nobody would know who I am. The anonymous whistleblower is the one who's able to force the most focus on the issues. At the same time, had I done that, it would have set off an extraordinary witch hunt. People would have been unfairly implicated as aiding and abetting; they could have suffered legal liability. Revealing myself helped keep focus on the fact that this was real. But it also allowed the media to focus on me.

NOSSEL: Let's stipulate that there was going to be a face at the forefront of this campaign. My question is trying to get at the fact that it's your face, it's you, it's your line of thinking, your reasoning, your personality, and how you think that has played out in shaping the effectiveness of your message.

SNOWDEN: The fact that I don't really like to embrace the media, I don't like the story to be about me, makes me a less than ideal messenger because, as we discussed earlier, the government sort of owns all the Sunday shows, and if you wind the clock back to June 2013, every Sunday they had a parade of officials who would be out there and they'd mislead the public in concrete ways that I could have quite easily disproved, and shown that these were misdirections. Intentional mendacity. But I felt that this would make it more about me. Maybe I was overcautious; I tried to back out of it and let there be some other face. Let somebody else come and argue these issues. But the result was a vacuum where they smeared my character repeatedly for a number of months (it's still going on, but on a much lower level). If there had been a different person in my shoes who made the same decision but had a different personality, who was a little more media-hungry, who wanted to engage, to go talk to George Stephanopoulos, they would have been more effective in pushing back, they could have more quickly corrected the record when officials made false statements in defense of these programs.

NOSSEL: Given how motivated you are, why not overcome your natural reservations and go mix it up with George Stephanopoulos?

SNOWDEN: I think it comes down to personality. You're asking why I didn't become a long jumper instead of an engineer. Sure, in hindsight I can say maybe I should have done this, maybe I should have done that, but on balance, when I look back at things, I think it worked out really well. It did benefit the public in a clear, broad way, and if I had to go back and do it again, I'm not sure that I would change things.

NOSSEL: You painted a pretty optimistic picture of how things are going in terms of surveillance reform and the momentum that you see to address the changes that you're concerned about. You ground a good part of that in the technical fixes that you think will protect privacy even if legislation won't. But I wonder about the 2016 election, and what you think of the candidates' views on surveillance.

SNOWDEN: When he was elected, Obama could have said, "This surveillance program is a fundamental violation of rights—I'm against that. I don't care how you structure it, monitoring absolutely everyone in the nation without regard to criminal suspicion, without regard to any individual wrongdoing whatsoever, is a violation of the Fourth Amendment, and it's a violation of our human rights. That's not how we should be as people, that's not how we should be as Americans." Had Obama done that, he would have gotten moral applause. But as soon as there was any low-level terrorist attack or noteworthy criminal event, his political opponents would have said it was because of this decision.

We have to move away from the politics of fear that has enveloped our country for the last decade or more, and move into a post-terror generation: the politics of resilience. There will be crimes, there will be terrorist attacks; we will punish the wicked, but we will not elevate stability above liberty.

AUDIENCE: I wonder what you say to the many Americans who feel, "If my information is washed up in an enormous sea with hundreds and millions and billions of other records, I'm actually okay with that." Our sense of privacy and the acceptable level of government intrusion has been recalibrated, reset by the internet, by mobile, by your revelations. Even if we don't want to live in a security state, even if we want to move beyond a War on Terror paradigm, there may be a sense in which the American public has decided, "We can live with a lot of this."

SNOWDEN: I think that's changing. When we look at polls, we see that argument is becoming radically less persuasive than it was ten years ago. Arguing that you don't care about privacy because you have nothing to hide is like arguing you don't care about freedom of speech because you have nothing to say. It's not really about having something to hide, it's about having something to lose. When we're talking about rights, we're talking about relative power within society. These people do not realize, necessarily, consciously, what they're arguing about, because it's an abstract idea, and they're making an emotional argument without following it to its logical conclusion. They're saying it's okay for a government or other institution to have total power in society. Mass surveillance is a totalitarian power by definition. It monitors everybody's private communications, everybody's private records, their private lives in society. We don't let federal agents have a tour our home when we leave for work every day simply because it would give them an advantage in investigating crimes. Of course it would. They would find evidence of drugs, of fraud, of tax evasion, whatnot, if they had the power to go through everything.

In the digital realm, because it is invisible, it's very difficult to demonstrate wrongdoing, and to hold violators to account. The NSA's own records show they violate law or policies thousands of times in a single calendar year. Even if these policies are implemented by well-meaning people, they will not only be abused, they will be dangerous. If people do agree that we should embrace mass surveillance, that they don't care about the right to be left alone, that decision is fundamentally public in nature. The problem, revealed in 2013, was that this decision had been made *for* us, without our knowledge, without our consent. The programs had been put in place in secret and were being used against us, and in our name.

These policies are not passive. They're invisible, they're constant, these are things that are monitoring you all the time. People say, "It's just metadata, it's getting a copy of your phone records and getting an itemized phone bill." That's not at all what it's like. It's a record of every book you've ever opened, every library you've ever visited, every home you've ever visited, every person you've ever talked to, every cellphone tower you've ever passed, every method of transportation you've used. It is a perfect record of every private life. That is what metadata reveals, that is what bulk collection or mass surveillance produces. Ultimately, it's not really about surveillance. It's about the balance of power within society. It's about whether we, the private citizens, stay protected. The government is not supposed to know a lot about us. That's why we're called private citizens. Public officials are supposed to be transparent: We're supposed to know a lot about them because they wield privilege, influence, and power to the most extreme degree within society. Privacy is intended not for these people; privacy is for the powerless. And if we do not protect it, we will not have it.

"Last time I checked, no real spy goes to the press with what they know."

A conversation with Thomas Drake,
Jesselyn Radack, and James Risen

JAMES RISEN: The Bush Administration issued me a subpoena in January 2008, and I thought that when Obama got elected the case would disappear. In July of 2009, the judge issued a very brief order saying, "I see that the grand jury in this case has expired, and I give the government ten days to decide whether to pursue this further." It was an invitation to the Obama Administration to let this drop. All they had to do was not do anything for ten days in July 2009. Instead, they immediately told the judge, "No, we want to continue the subpoena." The judge said, "You can't continue the subpoena, because it was issued by Attorney General Mukasey of the Bush Administration. You have to get a new subpoena." So they did. I kept getting subpoenaed and the judge kept siding with me. Finally, the Obama Administration took the case to the Fourth Circuit Court of Appeals, and they argued before the appeals court that there's no such thing as a reporter's privilege. That was the official position of the Obama Administration, that there is no such thing as a reporter's privilege or a shield law, or any kind of protection for confidential sources.

They won the appeal, and I took it to the Supreme Court and lost. At that point the only thing I was able to do was refuse to cooperate, though I had no legal recourse. Finally, the Obama Administration relented, only because they were getting bad publicity. They had won legally, but finally they decided not to force me to go to jail after I refused to testify.

This administration has extended and continued most of the Bush Administration's national security policies. If you are going to continue waging the global War on Terror the way George Bush did, you have to suppress dissent, and you want to keep operations secret. You can't let the public know about things like bulk data collection of all the phone calls in the United States. So the crackdown on whistleblowers and reporters seems to be part of a larger national security policy.

JESSELYN RADACK: The Obama Administration—which I campaigned for, contributed to, and voted for—has been far worse than Bush. As an attorney at the Justice Department who blew the whistle on ethical misconduct in the case of a terrorist suspect, I was put under a federal criminal leak investigation, referred to the state bars in which I'm licensed as an attorney, and put on the no-fly list. But I was never indicted. That didn't happen until Obama. Nine different people have been indicted under the Espionage Act for non-spy activity, and seven of those people are classic whistleblowers.

During his tenure at the Justice Department, Ashcroft had an anti-leak task force. Despite Obama's rhetoric that whistleblowers are courageous and patriotic, he came into office weak on national security and intelligence, and I think he was captivated by the CIA and dazzled by the secrecy. It's very easy to get wrapped up in the power. That doesn't excuse it at all: He's been worse than Nixon.

RISEN: I look back to the Valerie Plame leak investigation, which led to Patrick Fitzgerald, who was then an independent prosecutor, issuing subpoenas to a lot of reporters. He was given extraordinary power as an independent prosecutor. He could issue subpoenas without getting the attorney general's authorization (which is usually required for media subpoenas). He broke an unspoken agreement that existed between the press and the government for about thirty years, in which the government would look the other way and tolerate leaks. Fitzgerald's overzealous investigation of the Plame case convinced the Justice Department they could subpoena reporters and prosecute leakers, and the political damage wouldn't be that bad. Prosecutors at the Justice Department saw Fitzgerald become a star, and that became a model for the future.

THOMAS DRAKE: I would agree the Obama Administration is far tougher on whistleblowers, because although the Bush Administration criminally investigated me, it never led to an indictment. There was a draft indictment, but they withheld from crossing the Rubicon.

Obama has now presided over the most draconian crackdown of any administration. He saw a way clear—largely behind the scenes, but also with pressure in Congress and a lot of leaking to the press—to codify much of the policy of the Bush Administration and to institutionalize it. It's revealing that in one of his appearances, he spoke about a "legal framework." Last time I checked, the only legal framework the president is obligated to preserve, protect, and defend is the Constitution of the United States.

How ironic is it that someone like myself, who took an oath to defend and support the Constitution, would become criminalized by the Obama Administration for calling out criminal wrongdoing on the part of the government? And that Obama actually looked backward to bring forth investigations from the Bush Administration and prosecute? And using the Espionage Act to do so? Last time I checked, no real spy goes to the press with what they know.

ON THE BREAKING POINT

RADACK: Our first prisoner in the Afghanistan War, a guy named John Walker Lindh, was later dubbed the American Taliban. Not only did they fail to Mirandize him properly, but the attorney general claimed that if Lindh had had a lawyer, he would have been permitted that lawyer—which was a lie, because he did have a lawyer—and that his rights were carefully, scrupulously guarded, which they weren't. He was tortured, he was kept in a shipping container for days with no food, with bullet holes in his leg, tied up with duct tape, bound, gagged, blindfolded, completely naked. It's what we saw at Abu Ghraib four years later, but this was the first instance of it. That was enough to push me over the line. You hear your agency lying, and you think, "Okay, it's the attorney general's prerogative to take the position he wants." But when someone's facing a bunch of death sentence counts—I felt I couldn't live with myself if I didn't speak up, and someone was put to death because I kept my mouth shut.

DRAKE: It comes down to who we are as Americans. It comes down to rule of law, and whether or not you can have license over yourself under the rubric of security. This is something that Frank Church warned the nation about in 1975, during the conclusion of a set of hearings that revealed that instruments of national power were being used to violate the rights of Americans on a large scale even for the technology of that time. It's extraordinarily tempting to use technology for other purposes. That's what I was confronted by. I can say this in very stark terms: I was seeing the subversion of the Constitution. I was watching the wheels coming off a government which I had taken an oath to support and defend against all enemies foreign and domestic. What I saw was an alien form of government arising from within.

9/11 was indicative of a government that had failed to keep people out of harm's way, and which then used that as a frame to justify licensing unto themselves all sorts of extraordinary powers. Those are emergency powers. Those powers aren't granted in the Constitution. No one declared war, but suddenly they were acting like the whole world was a battlefield, including the United States of America. In those first few days and weeks after 9/11, I confronted the lead attorney in the Office of General Counsel, who said, "Tom, you don't understand. The White House has approved that program (the mass surveillance program called Stellar Wind). It's all legal." As soon as he said, "It's all legal," I remembered being a teenager in the Nixon era. "Well, hey, if the president says it's okay, it's not illegal." Really?

That was my moment of truth. Most people would think, "You didn't make the decision, you weren't the one to authorize it, you weren't the implementer. Why would you get in the way?" People don't realize that the vast abuse of instruments of national power in the '50s, '60s, and '70s, culminating in the '70s, led to a series of reforms, to standing committees on intelligence in the Senate and the House. It led to the Foreign Intelligence Surveillance Act of 1978, which was updated five times prior to 9/11 to keep up with the technology and the times. A twenty-three-year legal regime, which had hot-pursuit options built in, where you could actually go after a target, a true threat to public safety, and then go back to court for the warrant, was tossed overboard after 9/11. If rule of law doesn't matter, if the Constitution doesn't matter, if the principles and practices under which the country is founded and has evolved, if the arc of history bending toward justice doesn't matter, then what matters? The cornerstone of all this is the First Amendment. This is what's troubling, and what is a direct threat to our special form of democracy, the constitutional republic: when you have a president who is more than willing to use instruments of national power to erode the foundation of the country.

ON RETALIATION

DRAKE: I was confronted by a number of things going on in NSA after 9/11, and I researched what was available to me in terms of channels, because I recognized that no matter which channel I utilized, I would eventually be exposed. We're talking about high crimes and misdemeanors as defined by the Constitution, multibillion-dollar fraud, waste, and abuse. We're talking about covering up intelligence NSA had that could have stopped 9/11. NSA clearly had reasons to keep this out of people's inboxes, and reasons to protect itself even from others in the government. So when I confronted my supervisor, as well as going to the office of general counsel and the inspector general's office, and later became a material witness and whistleblower for two 9/11 investigations, I recognized that if NSA wanted to, even though I was a senior executive, they could make life extraordinarily difficult.

I knew that I had touched the third rail by going to the press. As soon as you make that contact, you've crossed a line in terms of national security, particularly in the hyperinflated fear and paranoia generated post-9/11. So when I decided to go to the press in February of 2006, I knew that not only could I get fired, but that the government—if they wanted to—could do what they did to Daniel Ellsberg. I knew that then. But for me, it was necessary at that point, because all the whistleblowing, through every channel that existed, had come to nothing.

Then they said, "You have no job anymore." They reorganized the department of engineering, and when they finished reorganizing, I had an office and a flag and a computer, and nothing else. I found a job at the National Defense University, which was a lateral arabesque to another position, another function, because I was an "insider threat." I had become the dissident as far as NSA was concerned. If you become a dissident within that kind of institution, the white blood cells kick in, culturally, and they get rid of you. If you disagree, if you question authority, then you might find yourself facing prosecution. And I'm one of the public figures. What you don't hear about are the dozens and dozens of people—actually, going into the hundreds, even into the thousands in terms of people caught up in these investigations—whose patriotism, loyalty, and character were all questioned.

ON PROTECTING SOURCES

RISEN: Whistleblowers face much greater dangers than reporters do. We in the press, the government can make our lives difficult and can make our job hard, they can threaten us and try to put us in jail, but it's far worse for sources and for whistleblowers like Tom. That's the first thing we in the press have to recognize: We are doing a poor job of finding ways to help sources and whistleblowers. We're basically doing nothing. One of the problems is that cases like mine, involving reporters, generate a lot of sympathy in the press, because it's one of our own. Whistleblowers and sources don't get the same treatment from the press; they don't get the same treatment from the government or the public. The main thing I wanted to say today is we have to find a way to change that. We should start thinking about how to protect sources better, how to find ways to change the dynamic that now exists. My life has been made more difficult by the Obama Administration, but I can still do my job, and people still want to talk to me. In a way, it's been good advertising. People know that I refuse to testify, they know that I can be trusted.

The other thought I had about the way we treat whistleblowers in the press—and it's a criticism I've had for quite a while, because it's a criticism I've lived—is that when there's a story about a whistleblower and there's a leak investigation, we in the press treat it like a cop story. We treat it like a criminal investigation: "Who is the leaker? Who is the source?" It becomes a police procedural story very quickly instead of a story about "Is this the right thing for the government to be doing?" That gets to the larger issue of whistleblowers, that it's very difficult for the government to accept that a whistleblower can be someone who disagrees with a policy. The government's definition of a whistleblower is just someone who sees waste, fraud, and abuse. They have this very micro view of what's acceptable whistleblowing. Someone like Edward Snowden, who sees a giant program that nobody knows about, is not considered a whistleblower, because that policy was authorized by the president.

RADACK: At an event for journalists not long ago, they did a poll of how many were using encryption, and it was only a handful. You can't just say that encryption is source protection; that is a myth, and a dangerous one. Source protection needs to be more than that. Journalists don't want to get lawyers involved because they're under the misimpression that we're going to say, "No, you can't put anything on the record, and no, you can't say this and that," but I would argue that we know how to keep people safe. At least in my practice, I'm glad to bring people to the media, because by and large, I think the media is more a help than a hindrance to the whistleblower. But the only people who are using encryption less than journalists, maybe, are lawyers! That's why, in my new whistleblower and source protection program, tech and encryption is part of it, but I also know that Jim Risen does this old school, and he's one of the greatest reporters in the country.

There's something to not relying so much on intelligence. I mean, that's what we're faulting the government for, that they have overrelied on tech instead of good old detective work, gumshoe human intelligence.

That's why, in spite of all the surveillance, we failed to detect or prevent the Boston bombing, Denmark, or *Charlie Hebdo*. It hasn't worked. More technology makes it easier both to blow the whistle and to be caught. To say, "Well, it's all because of technology," absolves the government of responsibility for the prosecutorial discretion it has to ruin people's lives. It's like saying Obama is in a self-driving car, and therefore the car just drives wherever it wants, and the government has nothing to do with this. The government has everything to do with this.

THE TRANSPARENCY PROJECT

Alissa Nutting

After college, Cora found it hard to get a well-paying job. Amid stints as a waitress, a bartender, a barista, she came across a few medical testing gigs at a local research facility. Usually, these paid a few hundred dollars and required her to put a cream onto her skin that sometimes caused a rash and sometimes didn't, or to put drops into her ears that caused variable levels of itching and/or burning and then required her to rank the intensity of itching and/or burning on a numerical scale.

There were many things in life that Cora found difficult, like choosing which scent and brand of dishwashing soap to purchase. If all bottles of dish soap cost the same amount of money, were all the same size and color and merely differed in fragrance, it would still, she felt, be a very hard decision, because there were many fragrances and they weren't even in the same fragrance category: There was citrus, floral. There were atmospheric titles like "Ocean Breeze" that inspired their own line of thought and questioning altogether (for example, which ocean? How strong a breeze?). But other tasks, such as being at a given place at least fifteen minutes prior to the time when she actually needed to be there, had never proved to be a struggle for Cora. The researchers noted and appreciated this, and it led to her being offered the Transparency Project.

The Transparency Project was not a one-day test but a hired permanent job that would last until her natural death. When the leader of the research team said the word "natural" in the phrase "natural death," he emphasized it in a very unnatural way. Each year, her paid salary would be the previous year's average salary for all full-time workers in the city where she lived, in addition to a generous benefits package. All she had to do in order to receive this money every year until her *natural* death was come into the facility for monitoring and testing two days a week, eight hours per day. And have the operation. She could travel up to six weeks of the year, provided she allowed a monitor to meet her at a nearby hotel room for monitoring twice a week during each week of travel. If she were ever injured, comatose, or unable to come to the facility for any reason despite being alive, she would allow them to come to her for the monitoring. There would be legal documents outlining this permission. She would sign them.

The operation would remove all existing skin and fat from a front section of her torso, starting at the top of her ribs and ending at the top of her pelvis. Her blood and muscles would be infused with a harmless solution that would allow them to become transparent under selective wavelengths of light, including daylight and fluorescent lighting, allowing researchers to easily see through to her internal organs. Her skin in this region would be replaced with a clear, waterproof polymer film; when she wasn't at the facility, she could wear a flesh-colored silicone panel that would easily snap onto a sternum-mounted fastener. When they showed her the panel, she rubbed her hand across its surface carefully, like it was asleep and she didn't wish to wake it up. "What's this?" she asked them. It was a small brown nub in the sternum's center that had been designed to look like a protruding mole. It was the panel's release button.

The first few months after the surgery, she never released the panel on her own, and on observation days at the facility when the panel was removed, she felt very cold despite the fact that there was no drop in her temperature readings. She began bringing a blanket that she'd put around her shoulders when the panel came off. She avoided looking down at her own organs when the panel was off, mindful to keep her posture straight and her head directed forward or looking up at the ceiling. In order to do this, she pretended she was standing on the ledge of a very tall building, because she was very afraid of heights. Dropping her eyes would not provide a welcome view.

But gradually, this changed. The panel didn't feel like her own skin so much as a bodice or a giant waistband; she always wore the panel beneath her clothes in public, but when she got home she found she liked removing it and walking around her house in an open robe. The panel wasn't capable of sweating, but it often felt that way—despite being dry and even slightly cold to the touch, it felt like a tight shirt that was collecting her body's warm moisture; when she snapped it off and set it on her nightstand, always balancing it upright on its edge against a reading lamp, she swore her organs felt a rush of air. This wasn't possible, of course; the plastic layer that coated them wasn't porous or permeable.

But the psychological feeling was a pleasant one that she enjoyed. At first she only caught sight of her organs in accidental peripheral glances—the mirror, the reflective surface of the new chrome kitchen appliances she'd bought with her new salary. Then, day by day, the coils and twines of her insides became familiar geography, with patterns and symmetry that didn't threaten her sense of order but instead increased it.

The only sight that continued to give her discomfort was her beating heart. Not its image but its constant movement when she was at rest. Its pulsing reminded her of the way a digital alarm clock's numbers would flash repeatedly after the power went out and made her feel like an essential part of her needed to be reset. During each session at the research facility, a therapist came into the room at some point and spoke with her, and sometimes Cora would talk about the sight of her beating heart with the therapist. Usually the therapist had her speak directly to her heart, saying affirming sentences such as, "Heart, I appreciate you keeping me alive. Heart, I am grateful for your service." Other times, the therapist asked her to report any unpleasant dreams. Early on, she had a dream that she was at the beach in a bikini, and upon seeing her internal organs, a flock of gulls swarmed around her and tried to peck them out. Later she had a dream where she thought she'd woken up only to find herself standing at the foot of her bed watching herself sleeping. Her dreams were being projected on the skin panel resting on her nightstand, playing upon it like a video. It was the dream where seagulls attacked her at the beach.

Recently the therapist asked Cora to consider starting to date again. Cora replied that she'd never enjoyed dating, but that prior to the operation, it had been her habit to seek out companions for one-night sexual encounters. That she'd done this a few times a year prior to the operation, but had not done it since. "Then try finding someone and having sex," the therapist said.

So she joined an online service and tried. The first man declined to meet after hearing about the operation she'd had. The next said it was okay but changed his mind when she took her shirt off and he ran his fingers along the edges of the panel's thin seams. "I work on computers all day," he explained, "taking their cases off. Sometimes I get repair calls because the cases come loose and fall off on accident, all on their own." She assured him that it wouldn't, declining to admit this was possible if he pressed the release mole firmly enough by accident, or if she pressed it firmly enough on purpose. The third was fine with the operation and the panel's seams and even asked her to take the panel off and leave the bedroom light on. He wanted to watch her organs during intercourse.

They began having sex, but soon he stopped. "Sorry," he explained. "I feel like I'm watching a surgery in progress or something," he said. Cora was annoyed but thought it was better to pretend to be confused. She got ready to say, "There's no surgery," or tell him she'd had the operation over a year ago, except she got distracted by her dresser's mirror. She watched her heart beating again and again like an unanswered question, like a phone in her chest that would not stop ringing. "Hello?" Cora said. In the mirror's reflection, she could see that the man was no longer next to her in bed. Maybe he'd gone to the bathroom, or maybe he'd quietly left.

E PLURIBUS UNUM

Camille Rankine

by the glow of our equality I keep myself inside and when the sun
descends I descend and furtive in the dark I take
my difference for a walk

a woman stands before me with an open mouth as if to speak
I fix my face into position something kin to understanding
I have settled all my awe and weary at our living into

if it's all the same I say I reach my hand into the darkened day
as a woman turns her open mouth
closed and far away

and looking up we watch the kingdom on the hilltop
shift to rearrange and all the same
parts click and lock into their place

I move toward the living after all the only ones still here
for which I stand or rather have considered amity
and how much of a man am I what fraction

of me is mine and what belongs to a pattern
repeated endlessly I do not want to be afraid
I have decided I am not

afraid and in this hopeful state I call out to the living
we have been cleansed word has come down
from the hilltop we are one

people so we put our differences aside and quiet
our single mind we rest against the dark and let our eyes
adjust accordingly

THE FIRST PUNCH

Kazuki Kaneshiro
Translated by Takami Nieda

The door flew open.

Some kid, a first year by the looks of him, stood outside the door, his bloodshot eyes darting across the classroom. It was only a week into the new school year.

His eyes found mine and locked on. I decided to ignore him, and casually shifted my eyes back to the molecular anthropology book spread out on my desk. He stepped inside.

The lunch bell had just rung, so there were plenty of students still hanging around the classroom. They dug out what loose change they had in their pockets and began placing bets.

The kid strode past the lectern and made for my desk in the back row, slow and deliberate. I closed the book, slipped it in the drawer of my desk, and kept one hand inside the drawer.

The kid stopped in front of my desk. He loomed over the chair where I was sitting. I raised my eyes and looked up at his face. He was grunting noisily through his nose. The boy looked nervous, ashen, like a child before the start of a footrace. His chapped lips were pulled taut.

Hurry up and hit me already, I thought.

If he attacked me now, in my present position, I didn't stand a chance of winning. Yet in every altercation thus far, not one of my challengers had made the first move. Not a single one. And because of this, I was known throughout the school as the reigning badass with a 23–0 record.

The kid opened his mouth as if to speak, so I decided to cut him off. I was sick of hearing all the tired epithets.

"I'll make you famous," I said, quoting Billy the Kid when he drew his guns.

The kid said nothing, letting out only a shallow, puzzled sigh. He

Takami Nieda was awarded a 2015 PEN/Heim Translation Grant for her translation of Kazuki Kaneshiro's GO.

might as well have had a question mark floating above his head.

I grabbed the palm-sized ashtray hidden inside my desk, and in one swift move, pulled out my hand and sprang to my feet. His eyes clouded with terror the instant they seized upon the ashtray. He managed to throw up his arms in defense, but I was faster. Like I said, you really ought to get in that first punch.

I swung and smashed the ashtray against the bulge of his left brow—the supraorbital ridge, to be precise—with a little topspin. The skin there was thin and easy to cut.

Gshhh!

Right on the sweet spot.

As the kid staggered back, his left hand went over his brow. His eyes were out of focus. He was frozen in panic. I could've finished him there, but I waited. I wanted everyone in the gallery to get a good look.

Within seconds, blood was streaming from between his fingers. People usually react to seeing blood in one of two ways: lose the will to fight or pump themselves into a frenzy. I had no idea which way this loser would react and had no intention of gambling. I decided to finish him off.

I drilled him in the soft part of the knee, putting my full weight into the kick. The kid crashed into a couple of desks and went down on his side. After pushing my desk aside to make some room, I kicked him in the stomach, again and again. Not with the tip but with the top of the foot. A toe kick is harder to pull back on and it's liable to rupture the internal organs. Not to mention it doesn't make a sound. But with the top of the foot, it's easier to pull a kick, and a well-executed kick makes a *thwack* or *whump* sound, making it the perfect deterrent to scare away any would-be challengers in the gallery.

I stopped kicking. He was curled up like a newborn baby, trembling. A terrible feeling of sadness came over me. Damn it if this poor kid wasn't somebody's precious child.

After taking a breath, I slid my desk back to its usual spot. I put the ashtray in the drawer, took out a tiny bottle of adrenaline solution from my bag, and tossed it in the kid's direction. Just a little of the stuff would stop the bleeding. Honestly, this act of pity wasn't going to do me any favors in the future. The students in the gallery were sure to spread rumors that "Sugihara's gotten soft," which would bring all sorts of challengers like this kid out of the woodwork to take me down. But I think I'm in the clear. Today's trifecta of *ashtray, blood,* and *kicking* was a pretty good show, so by the time school got out, the story would have blown up into something like *brick, head trauma,* and *bawling.* If the story settled about there, they'd be too spooked to challenge me until the start of summer break.

The leader of the Black Liberation Movement, Malcolm X, put it like this: "I don't even call it violence when it's self-defense, I call it intelligence."

I hated violence as much as Malcolm did. But sometimes you don't have a choice. If someone strikes you on the right cheek, do you turn the other cheek? Hell, no. Some jerks will bypass the cheek and hit you where it hurts. Even when you've done nothing to deserve it.

I stepped past the kid still trembling where he lay and headed for the door. The daggerlike stares from the gallery were so sharp I could feel them against the back of my head. I spotted three 100-yen coins on top of the desk next to the door. Around the desk sat three students. I stopped and asked no one in particular, "Who'd you bet on?"

They looked down at once. I slid the coins into my hand and left the classroom. As soon as I left, I realized that this was the first time I'd spoken to them. We've been in the same class for three years.

I went to the cafeteria and bought myself some milk with one of the coins I'd just procured. Calcium is calming when you're feeling worked up. The cafeteria was pretty packed, but I managed to find an empty seat at a long table and sat down. The others at the table quit talking as soon as I sat down. This was nothing new, of course, so I punched the straw through the milk box and drank my milk.

Three minutes later, I was the only one sitting at the table. Once I drained the milk box, I made a game of knocking it over and re-standing it to pass the time. After I stood the milk box upright for about the twentieth time, Kato came and sat down across from me, a stupid grin plastered across his face. "I heard you took a wrench to someone's head."

So the current rumor going around involved a wrench. I shook my head. "It was an ashtray. You remember the ashtray."

Kato narrowed his eyes and stroked the bridge of his prominent nose with a loving finger.

I was admitted to a private all-boys school whose rating was about as high as the calories in egg white. But to someone who'd been educated in Korean schools and studied less than a year for the entrance exams, getting in meant as much to me as if I'd been accepted to the University of Tokyo.

One day about two weeks before the start of the term, I was summoned to the high school. I was shown into the office where the vice-principal and the teacher in charge of incoming first years asked me to "attend school under an alias so we don't have any problems." In other words, they wanted me to take a Japanese name and conceal my heritage, because going by my Korean name might get me bullied.

"I take pride in the name passed down to me by my ancestors. Concealing that name would be like throwing away my pride. I won't do it."

Actually, those words never left my mouth. I did as I was told. Why, you ask? Because ever since I announced my intention to go to a Japanese high school, my Korean teachers really laid into me. One teacher called me an "ethnic traitor." A turncoat. I've been called worse, but more about that later.

Branded an ethnic traitor, I decided to thoroughly betray the ethnicity to which I belong. Even though I'd agreed to go by a Japanese name, I had no intention of hiding the fact that I was Zainichi. Not that I was going to pop off about it either.

At least, *I* wasn't going to do it. But just as you might expect from a second-rate school, the teachers were second-rate, too, and they listed the name of my junior high school, which includes the words "North Korean," unchanged, alongside my Japanese name, "Sugihara," in the student register.

The first challenger appeared before me three days after the entrance ceremony. Korean schools have always been seen as these exclusionary karate dojos crawling with thugs. Full-contact dojos, no less. Needless to say, that was just a stereotype. There are plenty of tenderhearted guys who would rather spend the day in a meadow twining poppies into necklaces. Then there are the vicious types who find no greater pleasure than in fighting brown bears over spawning salmon in a raging current. I'd be willing to bet that Japanese schools have their fair share of both, but sadly, the bears in the Korean schools have been fed a belly full of prejudice. They keep feasting on that salmon, fattening up, growing more savage by the day. That frightening image is planted in the minds of the Japanese and takes root as the archetype for all Koreans.

So basically, to the students at my new school, I was a walking dojo signboard with the word "Korean" written across it. As in dojo yaburi—the practice of crashing a rival dojo and challenging its members to a match: If they beat me and returned with my signboard, they stood to score points with their pals. Stupid, I know, but then again I'm going to a second-rate school. What are you going to do? I'm not against that kind of primitive thinking. You either win or you lose, plain and simple. Everything made sense.

The first challenger turned out to be Kato. Kato was a bona fide badass, whose father was a top lieutenant in a criminal organization. I was pretty fired up, given how it was my first match, and I broke Kato's nose with an ashtray. Though I beat Kato easily enough, I was worried about what his father's crew might do to me. Turned out to be a whole lot of worry over nothing. Kato saw his busted up face as an opportunity to get plastic surgery on his nose, which he never much liked anyway.

After a while, Kato showed up one day with a sheepish smile, rubbing the ridge of his shapely nose, and said, "Thanks a lot." His father, who also seemed pleased with the result, said, "You gave my kid an upgrade," and took me to dinner at an expensive restaurant in Ginza. Kato's father was missing the pinky finger on his left hand.

Kato was the first friend I made in high school and the only one I could call a friend.

Kato stopped rubbing his nose and said, as if he had just remembered, "Today's my birthday."

"Well, you're not getting anything from me."

"I wasn't expecting it." Saying this, Kato produced a strip of paper from the pocket of his school uniform and handed it to me. "A ticket to my birthday party."

"A *party*? Who do you think you are?"

"Well, my old man's paying for it…"

"How much are you selling these things for?" I asked, referring to the ticket.

Kato smirked and said that it was a trade secret. Shoving the ticket in my pocket, I told him that I'd go if I was feeling up to it.

"There's going to be lots of cute girls there," Kato said. "I promise you a good time." He got up from his seat, and then clicked his tongue and added, "I almost forgot. My father wanted me to tell you to come by the house sometime."

"No, thanks," I answered. "I don't like yakuza. They bully the weak."

Kato made like he was about to cry. "C'mon, don't hate. He's only trying to make a living like everyone else. Besides, he really likes you. He's always going on about how you're going to be someone someday."

"All right," I answered. "I'll think about it."

A look of relief came over his face. Kato said, "I'll see ya," and moved off the table.

"Tell your old man I said hi."

The yakuza's son turned around, cracked a broad smile, and held up his hand as if to say, "You got it."

THE ALIEN CROWN

Lo Kwa Mei-en

The Alien Crown

The conquerers came and wrote the conquered into being
guilt-making, but pretty good in retro, plus, gosh, pretty to boot.
Um—so, "like" but "not": a citizen has a soul in his face of
fair; it's why *they* don't all look the same. Toddlers fumble thru
veni / vidi / verify but can recite my *name / number / allegiance*
except on multi-colonial awareness day, a false password we live.
Without anger, they beg, *poems work—don't you want to arrive?* God,
do I? When a conqueror sleeps in the collar of his hand, how
xenophobic pencils might shudder on a page of the domestic:
come be historic and sample a vowel: then write an index
yes is said to. Amen. But come the future. But say we climb
back on the boat. Say we pack the hull with work with angry
zephyrs—to, say it, their hell—and over it heave the extra
anchor, aim it to a future minus a canon the color of quartz—

The Alien Crown

The child in bloom may see the world, refracting
galaxy drowsy with seed, the opposite of a hole. That

stasis snuffs out like a life is still life. Seed in the plush

hull up to a sharp, tipping breath. The child is
running for the gold spaces of any given Sunday.

•

A police officer with a gun drawn is nothing like an enoki.

I know he is an unspeakable growth in the forest.

•

The child is a child. His mother is a mother.

•

Questions of intent are like aspartame to a honeybee raj
jerking on the hive floor: the world of a draq
pinned to the world by a world hoarding its own luck.

Kings in the capitol lift capital to the light like massive infants.

•

No child can stop

old men in their foyer and make a crown roll
loose alphabets past the rotting claw that will not let a child go.

•

No commander will ask a pistol to bend
and obey a demand for late bloom, new roots, and living loam.

•

Man's world must be just a wound hidden by a uniform,
loyal like a pauper dragon.

REVULSION

Horacio Castellanos Moya
Translated by Lee Klein

Glad you could come, Moya, I had my doubts that you would come, so
many people in this city don't like this place, so many people don't like
this place at all, Moya, which is why I wasn't sure you'd come, said Vega.
I love coming here toward the end of the afternoon, sitting out here on
the patio, sipping a couple of whiskeys, listening to the music I ask Tolín
to put on, said Vega, I don't sit at the bar over there inside, it's hot at the
bar, very hot over there inside, the patio's better, with a drink and the jazz
Tolín puts on. It's the only place where I feel at peace in this country, the
only decent place, the other pubs are filthy, abominable, filled with guys
who drink beer till they burst, I can't understand it, Moya, I can't understand how they so eagerly drink such nasty beer intended for animals,
said Vega, it's only good for inducing diarrhea, what they drink here, and
what's worse is they're proud to drink this nasty beer, they're capable of
killing you if you tell them the beer they drink is nasty putrid water, but
it's not beer, nowhere in the world would this seriously be considered
beer, you know it as well as I do, it's a revolting liquid, still they drink
it with ignorant passion, said Vega, they are so passionate about their
ignorance, Moya, they drink this nastiness with pride, even with a sort
of national pride, they're proud thinking that they drink the best beer
in the world, they think El Salvador's Pilsener is the best beer in the
world, not swill only good for inducing diarrhea as any healthy person
would think, instead they say it's the best beer in the world, this is the
primary and principal characteristic of ignorance, to consider your very
own swamp water the best beer in the world, if you call it anything other
than that, if you deride their swamp water, their nasty diarrhea-inducing
swill, they're capable of killing you, said Vega. I like this place, Moya,

Lee Klein was awarded a 2015 PEN/Heim Translation Grant for his translation of
Horacio Castellanos Moya's *Revulsion: Thomas Bernhard in San Salvador*.

it's nothing like those nasty bars where they sell that nasty beer they drink with such passion, this place has its own personality, it's decorated with some taste, although it's called The Light, although it's horrific at night, unbearable with the racket of rock groups, the noise of rock groups, which is perversely annoying to all those in earshot thanks to rock groups. But at this time of day I like this bar, Moya, it's the only place where I can come, where no one bothers me, where no one hassles me, said Vega. That's why I invited you here, Moya, The Light is the only place in San Salvador where I can drink and do nothing else for a few hours, between five and seven in the evening, for only a couple of hours, after seven this place becomes unbearable, it's the most unbearable place in existence thanks to rock groups, it is as unbearable as those bars filled with guys proudly drinking their nasty beer, said Vega, but now we can talk in peace, between five and seven no one will bother us. I've come to this place every evening since last week, Moya, I've come to The Light every evening since I discovered it, between five and seven, which is why I decided to meet you here, I have to chat with you before I leave, I have to tell you what I think about all this nastiness, there's no one else I can relate my impressions to, the horrible thoughts I've had here, said Vega. Since I saw you at my mother's wake, I've said to myself: Moya is the only person I am going to talk to, no other friends from school showed up at the funeral, no one else thought of me, none of the people who call themselves my friends showed up when my old mother died, only you, Moya, but maybe it's for the best, because none of my friends from school were really my friends, none of them saw me after school ended, it's better that they didn't show up, better that none of my old companions showed up at my mother's wake, except you, Moya, because I hate wakes, I hate to receive condolences, I don't know what to say, it bothers me when these strangers come up to hug you and act like intimate acquaintances only because your mother has died, it'd be better if they didn't show up. I hate to have to be nice to people I don't know, and the majority of people who give you sympathy, the majority who help at the wake, are people you don't know, you'll never see them again in your life, Moya, but you have to put on a good face, a contrite and grateful face, a face that's truly grateful for these complete strangers who have come to your mother's wake to extend their condolences, as though in times like these what you most need is to be kind to strangers, said Vega. And when you arrived, I thought what a good guy Moya is, and it's even better that he left so quickly, good old Moya, he left so promptly, I thought, I don't have to deal with any old school friends, said Vega, I didn't have to be kind to anyone, because hardly anyone attended my mother's wake, my brother, Ivo, and his family, a dozen acquaintances of my mother and my brother, and me, the oldest son, who had to come as quickly as he could from Montreal, who'd hoped to never return to this filthy city, said Vega.

But I don't understand what you're doing here, Moya, this is something I wanted to ask you, this worries me the most, how could someone who wasn't born here, someone who is free to live in another country, some-place minimally decent, prefer to stay in this shithole, explain it to me, said Vega. You were born in Tegucigalpa, Moya, you spent ten years during the war in Mexico, which is why I don't understand why you're here, how could it occur to you to return to live here in this shithole, to settle in a city that sucks you down more and more into its pit of filth. San Salvador is horrible, Moya, and the people who populate it are worse, they're a putrid race, the war unhinged everyone, and if it was already dreadful before I took off, if it was unbearable for my first eighteen years, now it's vomitous, Moya, a truly vomitous city where only truly sinister people can live, which is why I can't explain why you're here, how you can be around people whose greatest ambition in life is to be a sergeant; have you seen them walk, Moya? I can't believe it when I see it, it's the most repulsive thing, I swear, they all walk like they're soldiers, they cut their hair like they're soldiers, they think like they're soldiers, it's horrific, Moya, they all want to be in the military, they'd all be happy if they were in the military, they'd all love to be in the military so they'd have the power to kill with total impunity, everyone carries a desire to kill in their eyes, in the way they walk, the way they talk, they all want to be in the military so they can kill, this is what it means to be Salva-doran, Moya, to want to be like a soldier, said Vega. It's revolting, Moya, there's nothing that produces more revulsion in me than soldiers, as such I've suffered revulsion for fifteen days, it's the only thing this country produces in me, Moya, revulsion, a terrible, horrible, dreadful revulsion that everyone wants to be like soldiers, to be a soldier is the best thing they can imagine, it's enough to make you vomit. Which is why I say I don't understand what you're doing here, although Tegucigalpa must be more horrible than San Salvador, the people in Tegucigalpa must be imbeciles just like the people in San Salvador, in the end they're two cities that are too close to each other, two cities where the military has dominated for decades, infected, horrid, filled with guys wanting to be in good standing with the military, wanting to be around the military, anxious to be like soldiers, they look for the least opportunity to win soldiers over, said Vega. It's truly revolting, Moya, the only thing I feel is a tremendous revulsion; I've never seen such a bottom-dwelling race, so fawning, so happy to whore themselves out to soldiers, I've never seen anyone so possessed and criminal, with all the vocation of an assassin, it's truly revolting. Just being here fifteen days has been enough to know I'm in the worst place: Right now it's okay because there's no one here at the bar, Moya; I can assure you that after eight tonight, when the lunatics begin to come for the rock show, I can assure you, the majority will enter with a look in their eyes intending to make it clear they're capable of murdering you at the least provocation, for them the act of murdering you doesn't have the least importance, really they're hoping you give them the opportunity to demonstrate that they're capable of murdering you, said Vega.

You can't imagine the relief I feel knowing that I'll spend tonight in my hotel room, Moya, said Vega, I feel an enormous relief knowing that the week I have left here, I can spend locked away in my hotel room with the air conditioner on, without having to accompany my brother and his wife on all sorts of horrible outings that they insist I go on, to all these horrible places that supposedly Salvadorans returning home are so anxious to visit, these places they call "typical" that theoretically I should have missed during my eighteen years abroad, as if I ever felt nostalgic for anything related to this country, as if this country had anything worthwhile for which someone like me could feel nostalgia. It's stupid, Moya, a tremendous stupidity, said Vega, but they didn't believe me when I told them that none of it interested me, they thought I was joking when I repeated that I hadn't been nostalgic for anything, and they schemed to take me out to eat pupusas in Balboa Park, to do nothing more than eat these horrible fatty tortillas stuffed with chicharrón they call pupusas, as if they produced in me anything other than diarrhea, as if I could enjoy such fatty diarrhea-inducing food, as if I would want to have in my mouth the truly revolting taste of pupusas, Moya, there's nothing fattier, more harmful for your health than pupusas, nothing filthier and more detrimental to your stomach than pupusas, said Vega. Only hunger and congenital stupidity can explain why human beings here eat something as repugnant as pupusas with such relish, only hunger and ignorance explain why these people consider pupusas the national dish, Moya, listen to me closely, never let it occur to you to say they're dealing with a repugnant and harmful food, they'll kill you, Moya, keep in mind the tens of thousands of Salvadorans living in the United States always dreaming about their repugnant pupusas, so ardently desiring their diarrhea-in-ducing pupusas that now there exist pupusería chains in Los Angeles, said Vega; never forget that five million Salvadorans still in El Salvador religiously eat their plate of repugnant pupusas on Sunday afternoons, those fatty tortillas stuffed with chicharrón, this nasty greasy home-cooked meal they serve like the host on Vespers communion. The fact that pupusas are the national dish of El Salvador shows that these people have dull palates, said Moya, only someone with a totally dull palate would consider those repugnant fatty tortillas stuffed with chicharrón somehow edible, said Vega, someone like me with a healthy palate must endlessly refuse to eat such greasy nastiness, I once refused in such a way that my brother suddenly understood I wasn't joking, I wasn't going to eat those repugnant pupusas and perhaps this was the first altercation we had, in Balboa Park he began to reproach my ingratitude and what he called my lack of patriotism. You can imagine, Moya, as if I considered patriotism a virtue, as if I weren't completely sure that patriotism is one of many stupidities invented by politicians, as if patriotism had anything to do with these fatty tortillas stuffed with chicharrón...

DISCUSSING DIASPORA

Rashidah Ismaili, Cormac James, Abdourahman Waberi,
and Kerry Young, with Eric Banks

ERIC BANKS: You're all in some way exemplars of literary migration, whether it involves a move from Benin to the United States, from Jamaica to the U.K., from Djibouti or Ireland to France. I wonder if you might reflect on the autobiographical models of diaspora literature and the influence diasporic writers might have had on your work.

ABDOURAHMAN WABERI: I am someone who comes from the periphery of a periphery. Even in Africa, I come from the periphery. I come from a very small place called Djibouti, and I was born to a modest household where we speak only Somali. I was the first one who went to college and became literate in the francophone language of the place. At the age of twenty, I came to France without having the hustle and bustle that we have now, because at that time—which is going back to '85—it was quite normal for a young Djiboutian to go to Marseille, Paris, or Aix-en-Provence. I became African in France. This is the first irony, right? When I was studying in Caen, Normandy, for the first time I met a whole host of African brothers, friends, from Benin to Côte d'Ivoire. I was playing soccer with my friends and thought, "Okay, now I'm in the UN," because when I was in Djibouti, I defined myself as a Djiboutian. I knew about Europeans, but I was not aware of Ghanaians and Guineans.

In literature, I was also aware of coming from this periphery, that I was using the legacy of the forefathers within the francophone. Léopold Sédar Senghor was living not far away at that time, so I reached out to him, even tried to give him some poetry. I was aware that I was bringing something brand new, and I was thinking, in a very egoistic way, I had to

This transcript is adapted from a conversation that took place at the 2015 PEN World Voices Festival.

put Djibouti in a literary place, because we didn't have that. That was the birth of my writing consciousness.

CORMAC JAMES: For me, it's difficult to avoid Joyce and Beckett. In some ways, they set the blueprint for the relationship with the mother country, the mother tongue. Of course, that's complicated by the relationship between being Irish and speaking in the English language, a language that's been pulled from without. Joyce and Beckett are two very strong presences for any Irish writer, at home or abroad, and in particular for me, having in some ways replicated their migration from Ireland to France. Obviously their relationship with France, and with the mother country and the mother tongue, is at the forefront of my mind when I think about the subject.

KERRY YOUNG: Because I went to England when I was ten years old, I wasn't aware of being Jamaican. I wasn't aware of that until I went to England. So in a sense, I became Jamaican in England. When I started to read, the British writers didn't make sense to me; the Jane Austen and the Charles Dickens that were being forced upon me didn't relate to me whatsoever. As I grew, the writers whom I became attracted to were actually black American writers, James Baldwin and then later Alice Walker.

I decided to write *Pao* because I wanted to write a work of fiction. I had written a lot of nonfiction, and I wanted to prove to myself that I could write a work of fiction that someone would publish. That was the challenge, and when I considered what I wanted to write about, it was Jamaica, because that was still in my heart.

The subject of the first book, Pao, is fourteen years old and Chinese. In 1938, he goes to Jamaica and rises up to become the boss of Chinatown. The second book, *Gloria*, is about Pao's mistress, who's of African heritage. The third book, which comes out next year, is *Fay*, about Pao's wife, who's of Chinese heritage. I wanted to show the different Jamaicas: Gloria's poor Jamaica, the rich side that is Fay's Jamaica, and the ways in which those different communities interact. I also wanted to show that there is a Chinese community in Jamaica, which of course lots of people don't know, especially in the U.K. Everyone thinks of Jamaicans as being of African heritage. In Canada and here in the States, there are many more Chinese Jamaicans.

In terms of the question about writers, what Toni Morrison said about not writing for the white gaze influenced me hugely. In *Pao, Glo-*

ria, and *Fay,* I just wanted to tell our story. I didn't want to educate the white reader. It's written in patois, because I was just writing our story for us. The fact that it's had so much international success has come as something of a surprise to me.

RASHIDAH ISMAILI: "Onyibo" is a term in Yoruba, a derogatory term for white people, but it comes from the time of slave-getting. It now refers to people who put on airs, who have been to and come back. It is a put-down. I wrote *Onyibo* here; I don't think I could have written it in Africa. At the same time, what the two of you were saying about how you become, how your identity really comforts you and supports you in a strange place, you start to write from that kind of place. From *Onyibo,* which is one of my first publications here, to *Autobiography of the Lower East Side,* I wanted to talk about how I was on the Lower East Side in that environment, in that artists' community interacting with people, but at the same time being an observer.

The politics of the Lower East Side in the late '50s and '60s is very much a part of what was going on in the writers' community that later expanded to the Black Arts Movement, Umbra in particular. That was during the time when Patrice Lumumba was assassinated. It was the time of JFK.

I wanted to have world politics reflected on the locale of the Lower East Side, which already had its own historical, political life. You had tremendous numbers of anarchists and leftists. The old Jewish communist vanguard were on the Lower East Side. You had the Italian anarchists, you had the Russians. You could go on one street and hear Czech, then go on another street and hear Ukrainian, or Russian, or a polyglot of Spanish and English. All that was imposed on an area that was in fact an African village, because it was outside the municipality of New York City, and Africans could not be inside the municipality after dark. That's the kind of politics and culture that I wanted to show, so the Lower East Side isn't seen only as a place where European immigrants came. That happened, but on top of a structure that was already there, which is very seldom referred to.

BANKS: What years did you live there?

ISMAILI: I was there from '58 to maybe about '62 or '63, and then I moved to the "village proper." We didn't call it the Lower East Side at the time; this was Alphabet City. I was on 10th Street between C and D.

BANKS: Do you have an ideal reader that you're writing this book for?

ISMAILI: I have two readers in mind. The first is collectively my grandparents. That means that I want those old people who are unlettered, who are illiterate but not unintelligent, to read/hear what I'm saying because I believe that I am talking to them, and a lot of the language I am using, no matter what form it takes—whether it's French, English, or whatever—they understand and hear me. The second audience is primarily an audience of African peoples, and by that I mean both Africa and the African diaspora. Those are my primary audiences. It does not mean that people of European descent or Asian descent should not or cannot read and enter my work, but I believe it is important for people who look like me to see themselves in my work.

WABERI: Actually, I could have taken every word my sister said. I imagine someone I know, someone from my shantytown, because I was born and raised in a bidonville, the Djibouti shantytown. My first novel was entitled *Balbala*, and Balbala is a poor neighborhood. It's a shantytown of a shantytown, kind of. The funny thing is when I go back to Djibouti now, and sometimes as a "big man," I see someone who has taken a bus who has had a long ride and says, "I just want to say hello to the guy who wrote a book called *Balbala*." And I say, "Oh, funny," but having lived more than twenty-five years in Europe, it's as if I have I paid my first debt, have given back to Djibouti. I'm kind of freed from the dynamics of my country and my shantytown's legacy.

As I said, I come from this unprivileged background, no one was coming to it, no one even cared about reading French. It was just that I felt, as a young man from that area, I had to give back to them. When I was writing in Normandy, it was very tough, and I wrote a book on Rwanda, and it was the same thing. I wrote a book of testimony on the genocide of the Tutsi in Rwanda, and I was feeling the same kind of debt, that I had to give back to the people that shared their stories, because that was eight years after the genocide. People were giving me stories, and they were giving me very sound advice. They said, "You're a writer?" And I said, "Yes, I'm only a fiction writer." They said, "This is not serious, right? You have to be a historian. You can't trivialize our burden."

I became aware that I had to take my job more seriously. I had to say, yes, I have done the testimony from Djibouti, but now I'm in different territory, a territory where the lives of almost a million people have been claimed. I'm not a Tutsi or a Rwandan, but at the same time, people have shared something with me, saying with meaning not to trivialize their burden. They were saying to be a historian, or at least have the seriousness of a historian, and maybe the lightness of a fiction writer.

BANKS: Kerry and Cormac, in both your books, you have provided interesting research notes in the back, or at least a bibliography to help the reader better understand what you're writing about.

YOUNG: I wanted to place the characters in their context, in their time. *Pao* starts in 1938, which is when the first political party, the People's National Party, was established in Jamaica. It runs through when we got the vote, the West Indies Federation, then independence, the first Manley government, the second Manley government, up to when Edward Seaga became prime minister. That period was an important turning point, politically, for Jamaica. I wanted to get all those historical events right and provide references; when you've done the Ph.D. and all the rest of it, there's a tendency to want to put the references in to help the reader understand what was happening. We don't, as human beings, exist in a vacuum, we exist in a particular political, social, economic context, and that context affects our lives and the way we see our lives and the decisions that we make about our lives. I wanted to contextualize the people.

JAMES: That also comes back to the notion that to fictionalize is to trivialize. That it's just telling stories, and it's somehow a lesser form of conveying information—which of course is not true at all. Often it's a more complex means, because it renders the experiences that can't be given in a fact-based, historical account.

Some of you were talking about being in a home or culture away from your origins and the feeling of being slightly outside, an observer. You're participating, but you're maybe also pretending. You're seeing—with maybe a slightly more objective eye—certain things that people who have grown up in the place wouldn't be aware of.

When you go back to visit, you still have that sense of being an outsider, an observer. You're going back to the place where you grew up, you're dealing with the people, your friends, your family, yet you're behind a pane of glass. That notion of going away, of leaving the cultural context that you grew up in, isn't always a negative thing. You leave your culture and the social structure that formed you, and you also leave your family and friends. Sometimes you need to get away, to stand back, to turn around, and then from that position describe with a little bit less love or investment. Often it's the people who go away who paint the most telling portraits.

YOUNG: I had an interesting experience recently. I went to England at the age of ten, and I always felt as an outsider, as an observer, in England. When *Pao* came out, interviewers asked me why I always refer to Jamaica as home, even though I've been in England a very long time. They asked, "At what point will you call Britain home?" and I said, "When the British stop asking me where I'm from."

But recently I went to China on vacation. I don't know whether it was because I'd written "writer" on the visa application, or because, if you Googled me that week, you would have found something like, "Kerry Tells Chinese Government to Stop Persecuting the Five Feminists They've Got in Prison." I was horrified when I saw that (it turned out to be John Kerry). Whether or not that was an influential article, I picked up the attention of the Chinese police. It's terrifying to be under that level of surveillance when you think you're on vacation, to be followed to the extent that we were followed, room searches, all sorts of things. They didn't interfere with us, but we did have the feeling that we'd planned our itinerary and were being kept on that itinerary as we went down the country and eventually flew out of Shanghai. We were constantly aware of the surveillance. When I got on my flight in Shanghai, I realized how much having that British passport had helped me feel safe in that set of circumstances. I kept telling myself, "They can't actually do anything to me because I've got a British passport."

I think since then—that was three weeks ago—my sense of my identity as Jamaican and as British has changed. I think the next time I'm asked the question, "Why do you always call Jamaica home and you never call Britain home?" I'll have to have a different answer, because it was the British passport, it was being British that made me feel safe. If I'd been traveling on a Jamaican passport, I don't think I would have felt safe in the same way.

WABERI: If I had not gotten out of Djibouti, I would not be the same guy. When you are inside, you cannot voice the difficulties. The fact that we, all of us, have been living outside, we became outsider-insiders—if you want to talk about the ethnologies here. I call that the camerial eye. I can see from inside and outside at the same time, this gymnastics. I am the one who has written the most on Djibouti, and at the same time, some of the officials from Djibouti consider me one of the enemy, because I also say that it's a dictatorship, it's a hell-place. I couldn't even go back to see my mom. It's sometimes exhausting to have this camerial eye.

One last thing that I will say: You choose your own family. When I was a student, I had a huge love for what I call my two Edwards, Édouard Glissant and Edward Said. Those two Edwards were my grandfathers. If I had just remained in Djibouti, I would have never known my two Edwards. I chose them because they were on the path of this complicated, postmodern, cosmopolitan, difficult life: We are all from certain places but we are all from, at the same time, the same world and the same humanity. We forget that we have some huge commonalities when we are always talking about our small differences.

SISTER (1990)

Amber Atiya

she not short, not tall, snickers
brown, live in a room, walls
kinda white, kinda yellow
like her teeth. no tv. no radio.
her best friend goldie a gold
fish. she wanna teach me goldie
language. ma say no.
the pills make her sleepy
and fat and forget goldie
language.
if she can't talk to goldie
who she gon' talk to?
i say me. she say *you
just a kid.*
i say ma. she roll
eyes, place a pill on her tongue.
sis and goldie plan a trip
to the moon
say i should come play
pokeno, eat fluffanutter
sandwiches. if the weather
nice maybe they stay for good.
but how they gettin there?
and if i go
how i'm gettin back?
once i ask how she talk to goldie.
*same way that white boy
talk to pooh.*
sometimes

i just don't believe it.
then again.
sometimes i do.

THE MOTHER

Joseph Roth
Translated by Michael Hofmann

Yesterday the nineteen-year-old laborer Franz Zagacki was sentenced to five years in prison. He had tried to kill his mother while she was peeling potatoes, first with an ax, then by asphyxiation, and finally by stabbing her. Then, supposing she was dead, he robbed her of a wallet in her petticoats containing 2,200 marks, went to a tobacconist's, paid his debts, bought cigarettes, invited his friends and his sweetheart who had helped him plan the deed to a cozy get-together in the flat of the apparently deceased woman, and went out to have himself a fun day. The mother, though, did not die, and the son was arrested and taken to prison for questioning.

Yesterday the mother stood in court and explained that she had forgiven her son. No sooner were the wounds that he had dealt her healed than she was setting off to her son's prison, bringing preserves and other delicacies she had forgone. Even while she lay in hospital she was trembling for the well-being of her son, and if she had had the strength and if her lust for life had not prevailed when she was near death, then she would have remained quietly under the bedding in which he had tried to asphyxiate her, in order to spare him. What was her view of her child, she was asked. Nothing but the best. Oh, it wasn't his fault, bad company had led him astray, it's always bad company that's to blame. She didn't know anything about his girlfriend, he was impressionable, but when he was younger he had been a good boy.

The mother will now be able to visit her son regularly in prison. With trembling fingers she will pack up preserves for him for Christmas and the other holidays, and her old soul will weep for him and hope. And it will be exactly as though her son was not in prison at all, but at university or abroad somewhere, or in some other kind of place that is not easy to return from for professional or some other reasons.

The mother's day is full of work and painstaking, sometimes dirty labor. But between each thing and the next, the scrubbing of the floorboards and the chopping of the kindling, there will be a brief, secretive folding of her hands. And each time she sits down to peel potatoes, as when the ax struck her, she will cry from pain—but stronger than her woe is her hope, stronger than her pain her faith, and slowly from her love of the child, like young leaves from fertile soil, a kind of shy pride will sprout, without cause, she couldn't say why, not based on qualities, but simply on the fact of this boy's existence.

And each time she looks at the hatchet or thinks of it, a terrible day will loom up at her out of the past. And for all its terror, it's still weaker in outline and force than the other day, approaching, when her son will come home, upright, healed, and full of regret.

Full of regret? He has nothing to regret. The others are to blame, of course! Any moment the door will open, and he'll walk in. And even though it's five years, five lots of three hundred and sixty-five days, it could be any day.

SEDIMENTARY

Charles Patrick Norman

Years before we moved into the little white house
on the hill a road construction crew sliced off
the hillside edge to make way for the highway
as easily as Mama cut a loaf of sourdough bread.
Rains washed down the hillside and flowed into
a drainage ditch beside the road, revealing layers
of soil, sand, clay and limestone rock that provided
endless hours of fascination for three little boys.

Standing back and taking in the colored layers before me,
digging into interesting hues with a teaspoon, I uncovered
a broken chipped flint arrowhead crafted by
some hunter forgotten and long-dead, transporting me back
to a prehistoric Florida wilderness untamed by the
white man's machinery, imagined hunting with the Creek
ghosts for deer and squirrel, leaving behind no evidence
of their passing except for that sharpened arrow tip.

Another day I dug into a deeper orange clay and
found fragments of petrified wood lying where the
tree fell onto the forest floor eons before men came.
Then came ancient seashells embedded in a
mysterious layer of sand that tasted salt on my
tongue, tiny white periwinkles, clams and scallops
still perfect in their symmetry, sleeping
next to a darkened, stained shark's tooth I saved.

Charles Patrick Norman won third place in poetry in PEN America's 2015 Prison Writing Contest.

Our miniature Grand Canyon never failed
to reveal hidden treasures to my digging,
mementos I saved in a cigar box with old coins.
One day as I silently pondered my life and events
from childhood, digging deeply for lost memories,
I realized that my life was like that hillside, composed
of layer upon layer of sedimentary experiences
waiting for me to scrape away the sand with my spoon.

HOW TO DEAL WITH REGRET

Bob Morris with Ira Silverberg

BOB MORRIS: Arthur Miller once said, "Die with the right regrets." I'm not ready to die, but I've been thinking about death and regret lately. I guess it has to do with writing about what I did and didn't do for my parents when they were on their way out. But regret itself is pretty much a daily occurrence for me. It's kind of the Jewish fraternal twin of guilt. And we all know what a motivator that is, especially if you're a writer.

Regret, if you must know, is centered in the ventral striatum of the brain. It is seen by psychologists to be useful because it helps you make sense of the world, and it helps you avoid future negative behaviors. In other words, it can be an existential wake-up call that points you in the right direction. You regret rien? Really? Even if you're French, is that possible?

When my ailing mother had taken a terrible turn in the hospital, I was on a Scotch-tasting tour and didn't call home or e-mail, and I blamed the time difference, the lack of internet at all these Scottish castles where I was staying for black tie dinners every night. When my brother finally got me on the phone, he said, "If you don't come home and see Mom before she dies, you will regret it for the rest of your life." I didn't tell him that I really wanted to see Edinburgh before I came home. I did tell him that it would cost a fortune to get a ticket to come back two days early. Which was true, but I guess I must've been the guiltiest tourist in the United Kingdom for the rest of the week.

PEN America has asked me to do a how-to in five steps. Think of it not as a TED talk but a dread talk. How to deal with regret. It's in five steps, which I think we can all agree is better than twelve steps. And I'll drink to that.

This transcript is adapted from a conversation that took place as part of PEN's DIY series.

Step One: Do something regrettable.

That's easy. At least for me it was, as a son who was far too critical of my loving suburban parents. As a teenager, I once hit my father in the arm with my tennis racket during a tournament at our beach club. The entire club was watching, and I will never forget the communal gasp.

I once threw out a recliner from the den without my parents' permission. Put it right on the curb while they were away, because I thought it was tacky.

Who would do anything like this to these people?

Thirteen years ago, at the grave of my freshly buried mother, my father told me he had bought a plot for me so I could be buried with them. I told him no thanks, I didn't like the cemetery.

Step Two: Rationalize it.

Why did I hit my father with my tennis racket? Because he poached a shot and blew it, and he lost the game. I didn't want to play with him anyway. I had more important things on my mind, like pot and beer and cigarettes.

I didn't throw out the recliner because it was ugly; I threw it out because it was getting so rickety that it was dangerous.

This cemetery? I want to be in a quieter one, away from the highway, with some charm and maybe some hills and a poet buried nearby. Also one that's easier for my friends to get to—if I have any left after I've been such a nasty, judgmental person all my life.

Step Three: Have second thoughts, then ruminate and obsess.

Did I really have to hit him so hard with my tennis racket in front of everyone? Why didn't I just mutter something under my breath? Then, did I apologize enough so that everybody watching knew I was really, really sorry?

They look so bereft without their recliner. It's like there's a crater in the den where it sat all those years. And instead of replacing it, they're using a plastic chair from Kmart, which looks even worse. I miss that recliner. I wonder if I can get it back? Is it at the dump? Where is the dump anyway?

He offers me a gravesite with him and my mother so we can be together for all of eternity, and I turn him down? Why can't I say yes for once? Is it because I can't forgive him, because I can't forgive myself? Why is my default to him always no? What kind of son am I anyway?

Step Four: Try to resolve it.

I'm sorry, Dad, please forgive me. I didn't want to hit you with my racket in front of everyone. I don't know what got into me.

As an aside here, I want to get on the record the sad and regrettable fact that my rage at him went on for decades. And he never laid a hand on me, never drank, never touched me in any inappropriate places, giving me no real material to work with as a writer. He was just a sweet, flawed father who loved me so much.

Okay, okay, I'll buy you a recliner. Let's go look for one. No, not at Sears. We'll go someplace upscale, like Macy's. But the thing is, they were always at least $500 and that's a lot of money. And I wasn't able to shop with them because I never spent enough time with them because I didn't visit them very often because I couldn't stand the house or the town where I grew up.

I'm sorry, Dad. It's a nice offer: a cemetery plot for me. But it's just not my scene. This cemetery is so flat, first of all. The parkway is nearby, so there's a lot of traffic noise—and you know I'm a very light sleeper. Of course, none of this will matter since I'll be dead. So thank you for buying me a plot to hang out with you and Mom for all of eternity. I'll take it.

Step Five: Fail to resolve it and move on to write about it.

Writers are not the most therapized people. Maybe that's why we have to work out our struggles on the page, writing to understand ourselves better. Most of the regrets I've shared with you tonight, I've written about. Some I also resolved. And, in the end, my father knew he was loved, both my parents did. Although I never replaced that fucking recliner.

And by the way, I did buy a $1000 ticket to get my ass home early from Scotland to see my mother die, to see the last breath leave her. And because of that and because my brother had guilt-tripped me home—my wonderful brother—I don't regret as much as I might have about her death. As for my father, I still regret so many things. Not giving him all the time he wanted at the end. Not letting him show me the thirty-five different bank accounts he had with all this money he had saved for me, which actually made a big difference when he passed away. He deserved to be thanked.

Regrets are as regular as breaths. They tell us we're alive. But studies show that when you're older you don't regret as much. When you're older you tend to accept. And at the end, you look back at your life and what do you see?

•

IRA SILVERBERG: For those of you who don't know me, my name is Ira. I was introduced as a professional in publishing, but I'm also married to Bob. So I feel very comfortable having this conversation.

MORRIS: I don't.

SILVERBERG: "I sit close, shut my eyes, not wanting to see her another minute. And before I can stop, I find myself muttering, 'Are you going to die already?'"

MORRIS: He finds the most embarrassing part of the whole book. My mother was sick for a long time, and if you've been through this, you know death doesn't take two seconds or even two hours. It takes a long time. My mother had been hanging on for ten years, and we all thought she would go. But she was struggling and suffering and making us suffer watching her suffer, and at some point, that's what went through my head. "Are you going to die already?"

SILVERBERG: And today, when you hear that read back to you, do you regret having thought it, having written it? How does that work into the five steps?

MORRIS: I think that I was trying to give readers permission to feel the things they really feel and can't say.

SILVERBERG: Part of the endeavor in writing this book, I think, was about keeping your parents alive.

MORRIS: Since I don't have children of my own, these were my peeps, these were my primary relationships in life. I mean to come out of the body of two people and to have them love you unconditionally and see them go—yeah, I think I did want to keep them alive.

SILVERBERG: You and your brother have been in conflict probably for your entire life as a writer because your family has provided you with a lot of material. Who owns the material? Are you taking something away when you write about other people? Is it something that you think about when you're going through the process?

MORRIS: You know that in some cultures people don't want their pictures taken because they think you're taking their soul away from them. And I suppose that's true. It's really hard. My brother is very unhappy with the essay I published in the *Times*, an excerpt from the book. He had already read the manuscript and was unhappy with it, and I did everything I could to make it gentle without really changing the power of the book. And I understand. It's just that I don't know what else to do with myself. I don't know how to show both the conflict and the tremendous love I have for him. For those of you who are writers, I will tell you something: People who are written about actually are not patient for the arc of them redeeming themselves. I had to set up the conflict and then eventually he comes off as a hero, but he couldn't see that in the 1,200-word excerpt in the *Times* on Sunday.

SILVERBERG: How much regret do you carry about people?

MORRIS: Do you know who my next subject is? You, Ira.
 In some ways I wish I were such a good writer, that I was Jonathan Franzen, and I could invent such invigorating worlds and not rely solely on what I know and experience. And yet, this is all I can do. And I'm sorry for you.

SILVERBERG: I have nothing to say.
 As a publishing person, I would say you've written a book that is meant to speak to a generation, to speak to baby boomers about something bigger than your own experience. You went through it, you wrote it, but you do think about larger issues. And as I look around this room, I look at a lot of people who are dealing with issues around aging parents, transition in terms of their parents' lives. What advice do you have for people in terms of what they can do to go through what you went through and have just written about in this book?

MORRIS: He's fantastic, isn't he? See why I'm married to him?

SILVERBERG: I used to be in PR.

MORRIS: I think this is hard to advise, but if you can enjoy life as much as you know how, in any way you know how, in any way that works for you, it's going to affect your parents. Anything that you can do that makes you happy while you make them happy will make you happy. When it's over, you'll be inspired. Death, in some terrible way, is an opportunity for all of us.

SILVERBERG: A note about the grave Bob spoke of earlier: His dad offered me a plot as well.

THE SUDDEN TURN TO BIRD

Ishion Hutchinson

Their time under the pepper tree,
that love the sandflies make for mating water,
filling her apron with velvet brimstones;

the lane darkens with homing-mongrels,
and the white and scarlet necromancer's flags
sweep bright her excuse in his dreads,

pulling down riverbeds from out of the moon;
evening fastens on the hills turned bats,
voices lost in the canes, crisping, weightless

as lines rattling in an exercise book;
that blood-lint driven into the cardinal sea,
his glance under the flare of her eyes

molten by night itself that are blades
that ripple and jostle the hot rain
for tiny bridal bells, but she gleams, averted

to a violet silence beyond the branches,
heavy as the gully flooded with periwinkles
she ascends, spilling gems he couldn't track. Ever.

POMEGRANATE

Karissa Chen

Laila holds the wedge out to me, a honeycomb of jewels. Winking in the summer light. Capsules like love, like blood. *Here, Grandpa,* she says. Her chubby fingers slick with juice. Her chin dribbling.

I shake my head no. I say, *You eat it, xin gan bao bei.* My heart, my liver, my little treasure. She crouches in the grass, picking out individual seeds with her small finger, like she is scratching scabs. She rolls each one between her thumb and index. Eyes it, holds it to her lashes, tries to see through them. Red-tinged world.

Don't you like pomegranate? Laila says, face still flushed with delight.

Xin gan, bao bei, treasure, heart, liver. The night before I left our village, my mother held me close to her breast. I was thirteen, the top of my head just beginning to pass her chin. She smelled like flour and oranges. Elsewhere, boys only a little older than me were dying, bleeding, calling for their mothers, dead. I didn't know anymore who was doing the killing—the Japanese, the Communists, the KMT, my neighbors, my uncle, my father. My mother pressed me closer. *Away from here, you will be safe.*

Laila digs into the ground with a stick, a tangle of grass and dirt. She spits pomegranate seeds into the hole. They're white, stripped bare. Like tiny grains of rice. *I'm planting a tree, she says. Then we can eat all the shi liu we want.*

My body recoils, curling into itself. But I say, *Clever, bao bei.*

Shi liu, pomegranate. That last morning, my mother pressed a large one into my hands, the lone fruit birthed by the tree in our courtyard. A snack for the road, a wartime treat, red like luck, like happiness. I'd never held such a precious thing before. *Think of this as a school trip,* my mother said. The cart was filled with other children. An overcast sky. My mother stood by the road, hands wrung into her shirt. No matter what, come home, my mother said. *When you're fourteen, fifteen, sixteen, sixty. I will wait for you.*

Laila is counting the seeds she's collected in the hole. First in English, then in Chinese. What are you doing? I ask, and Laila says, I'm counting sixteen seeds. If I plant sixteen pomegranate seeds, they'll all grow.

Shi liu, pomegranate. Shi liu, sixteen. By sixteen, I am alone, motherless in Taiwan, with no way back to the mainland. Liu shi, sixty, and I am old, I am in America, far from home, I am watching my granddaughter pluck sixteen rubies.

I remember: My friend's mother had given him a hardboiled egg for the journey. Squeezed next to me in the cart, he rolled it along his thigh, back and forth. My mother smiled from the road, her hands pressing her elbows. She looked like the thin white birch that lined our village. I cupped the pomegranate in my palms, brought it to my nose. Inhaled its earth. I wondered if there would be more fruit by the time I returned.

Laila pushes dirt into the hole, pats it into a little mound. She sprinkles pith on top, a cracked red piece of rind.

That leather, that red-brown skin, that powder beneath my nails. I was hungry, I was thirsty, I couldn't wait. The cart began to move. The fruit split open to white membrane, crimson abundance, its juice wetting my fingers. I bent down to lick my hands, to slurp the sweetness.

Laila stands and brushes dirt off one hand, her other hand still holding pomegranate, her shorts stained red and brown. A few pods remain, standing out like ruby teeth. Shi liu like blood. Shi liu like home. Shi liu, trove of pain and blame. The cart was gaining momentum. My friend nudged me, said, *Your mother is waving*, but I was biting, savoring the burst of red honey on my tongue.

Shi liu, a torrent, swiftly moving away.

When I looked up, we were rounding the bend. My mother was gone.

Laila runs up to me, holding out the last of the fruit. *Grandpa*, she says. *Eat, eat*, I urge her. She shakes her head, looking back at the mound. *For good luck*, Laila says. *They won't grow unless you eat, too.* I stare at her, at her lips stained red. *Grandpa*, she pleads, her wrist shaking gently in my face, *I want them to grow*. Laila, her name sounding like coming, like arrived, like I am here. My mother's eyes, my mother's mouth. *Grandpa*, she says once more, and waits. Three seeds gleaming in her palm.

A PRAYER FOR WORKERS

Yusef Komunyakaa

Bless the woman, man, & child
  who honor Earth by opening shine
in the soil—the splayed hour
  between dampness & dust—to plant
seedlings in double furrows, & then pray
  for cooling rain. Bless the fields,
the catch, the hunt, & the wild fruit,
  & let no one go hungry tonight
or tomorrow. Let the wind & birds
  seed a future ferried into villages
& towns the other side of mountains
  along nameless rivers. Bless those
born with hands made to grapple
  hewn timbers & stone raised from earth
& shaped in circles, who know the geometry
  of corners, & please level the foundation
& pitch a roof so good work isn't diminished
  by rain. Bless the farmer with clouds
in his head, who lugs baskets of dung
  so termites can carve their hives
that hold water long after a downpour
  has gone across the desert & seeds
sprout into a contiguous greening.
  Bless the iridescent beetle working
to haul the heavens down, to journey
  from red moon dust to excrement.
The wage slave two steps from Dickens's
  tenements among a den of thieves,

This transcript is adapted from remarks given at "Prayers and Meditations" during
the 2015 PEN World Voices Festival.

blind soothsayers who know shambles
   where migrants feathered the nests
of straw bosses as the stonecutters
   perfect profiles of robber barons
in granite & marble in town squares
   along highways paved for Hollywood.
Bless souls laboring in sweatshops,
   & each calabash dipper of water,
the major & minor litanies & ganglia
   dangling from promises at the mouth
of the cave, the catcher of vipers at dawn
   in the canebrake & flowering fields,
not for love of money but for cornbread
   & clabber on a thick gray slab table,
for the simple blessings in a hamlet
   of the storytellers drunk on grog.
Bless the cobbler, molding leather
   on his oaken lasts, kneading softness
& give into a red shoe & a work boot,
   never giving more to one than the other,
& also the weaver with closed eyes
   whose fingers play the ties & loops
as if nothing else matters, daybreak
   to sunset, as stories of a people
grow into an epic stitched down
   through the ages, the outsider artists
going from twine & hue, cut & tag,
   an ironmonger's credo of steam rising
from buckets & metal dust, & the clang
   of a hammer against an anvil,
& the ragtag ones, the motley crew
   at the end of the line, singing ballads
& keeping time on a battered tin drum.

CALVIN D. COLSON

Merritt Tierce

Cal is a hustler. Maybe he's a type, maybe he's all over Chicago or At-lanta or some other bluesy black place like Memphis, where he's from originally. But his stuff works in Dallas because there's a lot more space around a black man striving here than in those other places. He was a king at The Restaurant. First thing he ever said to me was What are you doing crossing the guest like that. Don't ever cross the guest. I was new to The Restaurant and fine dining both, I was serving someone's salad with the wrong hand on the wrong side. I cared about him from that instant. Wanted to please him, got Velcroed to his there's a right way to do this. That was when The Restaurant was my life, when it was all I had, when I'd run away from her. I'd sleep till nine or ten, one big meal before the shift with the paper or a book. Alone, most always alone.

To do a good job at a table you have to care. Whatever show you're doing, wherever else your mind is, you have to put a twist of real on the very end of it. The people are waiting for that and if you don't pull it out they know and they don't like it. Cal did care, or at least he did that show better than anyone. Something in the way he leaned over people, touched their backs even though you're not supposed to do that, it was like they were in his home and he'd say Now what you want to do is put that first bite together with all of it, get you a little tomato, a little that purple onion, and the thing that brings it all together is you get a piece of that basil. Rub it around in that ba*sal*mic—mm! Mm. Tell me bout that.

He said a lot of words that way, slightly off. Mama gon' kick me to the curve if we touch, he'd say to me as we messed around on my floor in the afternoon. He had a bank job in addition to The Restaurant, some-thing one of his high-rollers made up for him. What he did there was try to look lively in a beautiful suit. Something from Bachrach. He could wear any color and he could put stripes and checks and prints together

Merritt Tierce was a finalist for the 2015 PEN/Robert W. Bingham Prize for her debut novel, *Love Me Back*.

and it would work because he was puffed up inside it like he was born to win. What I want to know is was that real.

In that restaurant all of us were off. Chipped. Everybody on the way to the curve. Maybe it's the same in a law firm, a nail salon, whatever high or low. Maybe that's just what it is to be alive, you've got that broken sooty piece of something lodged inside you making you veer left.

Calvin was profiled in a local newspaper when they did a piece on great Texas steakhouses. "Mr. Colson provides what he calls an 'old-school' dining experience, part service, part performance, and all professional. Ask for him at The Restaurant or you'll miss out on what fine dining ought to be," the reviewer said. Lissandri gave him a Rolex for that. If you read up on our level of service you'll find all kinds of uptight lists about not engaging with the guests, don't say your name, don't try to get call parties, don't push anything on the menu over anything else, be formal and anonymous and perfect. Cal broke all those rules and people tipped him outrageous sums for it.

One night one of his call parties didn't come through for him, this German-American guy Konstantin who brought in big business clients and left Cal somewhere between fifty and eighty percent on tabs that were never less than five hundred and could push up on four grand depending on how many guys he had with him and what he wanted out of them. On this particular night Konstantin was distracted or drunk when he signed the credit card voucher and tipped Cal $300 on $1,620, a figure that any one of us would have called a good night. Cal called it cheap and called it to Konstantin's face.

See, anybody else would have been fired for that. If a guest says to you Did we take care of you? after paying the bill the only possible answer is an effusive Yes, thank you for asking. Doesn't matter if they've been sitting there for two hours after the dishwasher left for the night, if they say Are we keeping you? the only possible answer is Oh no, sir, the place is yours.

Cal went up to Konstantin in the lobby where he was still working these Japanese guys, trying to get them all in cabs to the strip club, and made it clear he needed to talk to him immediately, and when Konstantin said What's up, my brother? Cal pulled him aside and opened the check presenter like he found a turd in it and showed it to Konstantin and said What is this?

Konstantin went all meek and said Oh did I fuck up? And Cal said I don't know Kon you tell me, but usually I see something closer to what I'm worth on this line. Is that what you think I was worth tonight? Something you weren't happy with? Because it seemed like all your guys had a great time and it seemed like they was going the way you wanted 'em to.

I'm not sure how he got Konstantin to think that the multimillion-dollar deal he had just closed succeeded in part because of Cal's excellent service but Konstantin rescribbled the tip in as $900 and said to Cal Is that more like it? I'm sorry, my man, I didn't mean anything by it. You know you're my guy here. And Cal had the audacity to shake his hand and say stiffly, still trying to be cold, That's what I thought but I was about to have to let somebody else be your guy here and Konstantin said I feel you, we straight?

You should have seen Nic Martinez doing his impression of Konstantin later in the parking lot. A Mexican doing a German trying to be black. Nic took a puff of Cal's one-hitter and passed it to Cal and then put his hand on Cal's biceps and said I feel you Cal my man my brotha my nigg we straight? You my homey right? You vant a couple more bills? You vant me to lick your nuts? and then he was laughing so hard, so crazy, he was leaning over in front of Cal, still holding on to his arm and coughing from the big hit he was trying to hold in and say at the same time Teach me how to get my own German, massa! Teach me!

Cal was holding up straight, letting a smile stay in his cheeks but looking at his pipe all serious, knocking the cache out, reloading. I know he knew his muscle was popping out strong with Nic hanging on him like that and he took pride in that and pride in his balls-out way with "his people," as he called his call parties. Ain't nothing to teach, he said to Nic, just got to be you and bring it.

He looked bronze with the streetlight shining on him, reflecting off his white undershirt. He looked the same color as Nic but he was really a goldish cinnamon. He said he was ochre, terra-cotta, and sepia, colors a former girlfriend, a painter, gave him. He liked that. He was always painting himself for me.

I mean did he really feel that way about himself though—the way he made it look in the bank suit, the way he made it look with Nic hanging on him. Where was the nugget you couldn't massage or change or put a pinstripe on and was it that confident. Was that kernel whole and well or was it sad, smacked out, lost. I don't know but I think a showman is all show. There's no secret—or there is, and that's it. Like when I asked Danny if that scotch rep Alyssa's tits were real and he said Yeah they're real—real fake.

Cal would have a little taste, as he called it, near the end of the shift when nobody was looking, a taste of Grand Marnier neat. Danny didn't care as long as the guests didn't see and Danny was usually drinking with him anyway. Cal's taste would become two or three tastes and then he would get so frisky, he would start touching all the women—servers, guests, the pastry chef—like you trail your hand through cattails out on a skiff. Pleased, enjoying the weather, nature.

One night after a few tastes he sat down with Doc Melton's woman—Doc wasn't there, and Doc was one of his big men, the ones who kept him on a sick and regular payroll of inflated gratuities at The Restaurant and threw in extras like Mavs tickets. Cal sat down with Cassandra Melton and he told me all about how he felt her up under the table, his fingers on her pussy lips, how fluffed and slick they were and how she sat into it delicately. He did this and after she and her girl-friends left, after he kissed her on each cheek, he came over to me and Danny where we were doing tequila shots at the corner of the bar. He was flying. Oh my Gawd, he said touching his fingers to his lips, that pussy. I can't believe I haven't been getting none of that. Why don't you Cal, I asked, why don't you just take it, always complaining about how long it's been since somebody took care of you at home. Fuck knows it's on offer for you everywhere you go.

No, he said. Can't do that. I'll touch me some titties and some pussy but I won't do that. Cal, that is such bullshit, I said, and he said You just say that because you want me to cross over. I do want you to cross over, I said, but it's still bull.

That was the summer Cal would come over to my apartment after he got off from the bank, before we had to be in at The Restaurant. Those were warm afternoons, my apartment toasting the Texas sun through big old perfect windows. I moved into that place when I saw the money I was making at The Restaurant. I bought that car too. You can make good money—high fives if you really push, low sixes if you're Cal—but you never lose the feeling that it's fragile, your connection to the money. That place I lived in after I first got that connection, it was small and expensive but it was clean and bright and everything was nice. The carpet was thick and new and Cal and I would scuffle on it every afternoon. His kisses. His face—so soft—Your face! I'd say—I take care of myself, Mami, it's what you got to do he'd murmur—his lips hot, fresh.

That much he allowed. But even if he was stripped down, his suit draped carefully across the back of the loveseat, his white V-neck undershirt tucked into his white boxer briefs, he wouldn't allow me to touch him. I reached and he said No, don't do that. We can't. Mama gon' kick me to the curve, I might as well move in.

Okay, I said, move in. I'm ready.

You not ready. You don't know. Why you always want more.

You want it too.

I do. No doubt. But you think we ought to touch outside of our want?

He was forty-four and I was twenty-two but he was in better shape. His waist as trim as mine, his pecs tortoise-shells, his quads modeling those boxer briefs. Before The Restaurant he used to train the Highland Park moms at Gold's. He still got up at four every day to do his reps—pushups, crunches, curls—before his daughter woke, then he'd make breakfast and take her to school. That was his time with her. Home late, never to bed before two or three in the morning, the office afternoon would fall on him like a tree. Him in that bank chair, sleeping upright in that suit.

So his excuse for coming over was he needed a nap. Only once did we actually nap—or he did, sleeping clean and gentle in his whites. I lay behind him, my hand on his thigh, breathing in the warm buttery smell of his neck, afraid to move, afraid to sleep and miss his sleeping in my arms, as if he were a comet, an eclipse, a papal visit. Not just a man pausing on me, a bead in his rosary.

But usually we rolled around on the floor, I listened to him talk, I begged for it, then I'd give up and go take a shower and he'd watch me start to finish, hand me the towel. Once he said You got a body too. Baby Rie-rie, lil M, look at those big nipples she got. Ugh. I could work with those big gumdrops and that bush. Real woman got a bushy bush like that, don't know what all this mess with some naked pussy lips is for.

Don't talk about it if you don't want it, I said. You're not for real. I'm for real. I'm ready.

You sure not ready for work, he said, looking at his watch, changing the subject. Looking at his fingernails. He got them buffed every Saturday, they were always shiny. His shoes too. He'd drop off one pair and pick up another. He had some military standards. He believed in the power of systems and order to manifest success. He believed in every cliched thing about the power of belief. He believed in believing in belief. I tell my baby she not allowed to use the word can't, he said. And he said I don't get sick cause I just refuse to. You tell yourself Oh I'm sick—he said this in a whiny puny voice, screwing up his face—you sure enough will be.

That swaggering, who knew it wasn't his belief in himself that made it all go. That it did work if you worked it. I was never that certain about anything. That's your problem, he said, you doubt yourself. You got to want it. I do want it, I said. Nah you don't. Not if you don't know you want it. What's that big dark thing behind you? he said, and I said I don't know, what, showing him I was impatient with whatever lesson was coming. That's the shadow of a doubt and you best deal with it right here right now.

What I wanted was some jack. Make that jack, baby, make that jack. Another one of his mantras. I got to get out there and make that jack, he said in the back station at The Restaurant, taking a long draw of his protein-ginseng-vitamin smoothie before heading out into the dining room with purpose. I wanted to know how to do what he did. Conjury. Turning dinner into livelihood, wealth, stability. My girl lived in a one-bedroom apartment with her dad, she slept on a futon in the living room. Cal's daughter lived in a giant suburban house with both her parents and took ballet. It's not that I even wanted a giant suburban house for her. I just wanted her to have something from me, anything better than absence.

Cal's daughter Elena, he got her in with this modeling agency. That was him—that belief in the most pressing uniqueness of his own life. No question. My daughter was beautiful too, at three she had flossy red hair down to her waist and strangers would use adult beauty words to describe her, like gorgeous. But I was always thinking something like *Nothing is really all that special.*

Cal was always thinking the opposite. And his daughter was what modeling agencies look for these days, a mixed-race child with fluffy hair and skin that one caramel Polynesian shade. She was tall, five feet when she was eight, with long delicate bones. Like Cal's having her in ballet and modeling from the time she was small made her that way or something. Like he willed it. He said Man, Maxine will not have that talk with her and I keep getting on to her, telling her it should be a young lady's mother has that talk. She's dangerous, she looks too old, boys gonna be after her in a minute and she so young inside still. I told Max she don't talk by her next birthday I'm gonna do it my own self, he said.

Max was Mexican, from Laredo. Cal said After my first marriage I knew the next one would be outside my race, but he never explained that or how he knew. His first wife Tamara was a black woman; they had a baby that was stillborn and took the marriage with it. Angeline, tattooed on his heart, scroll, script.

One afternoon before the afternoons ended he brought me a twenty-bag. He knew I'd gone back to coke even if I wasn't giving it up to everybody anymore. He couldn't believe I hadn't gotten pregnant or caught something during all that. Young lady, you got some kind of angel looking out for you, he said. But the main reason I was keeping it to myself was so I could have a chance with him, because I knew he would never go there with me if he caught the scent of anybody else. I let him think I was learning how to be a woman, as he put it, instead of just trying to get what I wanted from him.

He said the coke was from the Baron. The Baron was this Turkish guy who pretended to be Italian and dropped by The Restaurant once or twice a year. He'd show up like we'd been waiting for him and no one else through all that intervening time, each of us frozen in uniform, in place, until his presence disseminated some magic dust to make us come alive again so we could fulfill our destinies of serving him. The magic dust was some green and some white and all handshook. I'm sure Cal got the don's share of both and he told me he kept the bags to pass on to his people, just like he kept cigarettes and disposable cameras in his locker for when they ran out of smokes or got engaged. Once I even saw him fix a lady's dress with a safety pin he had in his pocket.

I never knew anybody who kept coke though, which is the main fissure in my Cal wall. It's a terrible habit but I tend to believe what people tell me, so when he told me the story of how years ago he quit using crack and coke I believed it. Then he gives me that twenty-bag and tells me he got it from the Baron and he's been keeping it under the floor mat in his BMW. I looked at him and thought You don't make your daughter breakfast and you're fucking Cassandra Melton and you didn't quit partying and you're not going to make it. I looked at him and looked away and I cut it into lines on top of a drawing my daughter made, the two of us portrayed as lean and grinning neighbors in one of those stick-figure sketches that seemed more a demand for normalcy than a depiction of the actual. This is the kind of obstinate I was. I thought it was bad form to lay it out on her little picture like that, like it seemed too obvious a send-up of my failings, like I ought to keep her effort sacred if only out of superstition. But that's what I wanted to face down—mine was an inversion of Cal's *just got to be you and bring it*. I wouldn't let myself look away from what I was doing and to punish myself for seeing it I wouldn't let myself fix it. Sometimes I would get home from work and I would get stuck in the car, just sitting there in the carport looking out over the steering wheel. An hour could pass as I watched the security light come on and go off as the bars let out, flushing cars up Greenville Avenue.

I did one line and Cal told me not to touch the rest till I saw what happened, said it was real shit and all I'd ever had was baby laxative because he knew I got it from the Mexicans at work. I don't know why I listened to him, that wasn't my practice usually, but within about thirty seconds my brain had melted. Why did you just do that to me, I said, sounding to myself like the gigantic demented rabbit in *Donnie Darko*. Why did you do that why did you do that why did you do that, I said. My face was falling apart. My face is falling off, I said to him, my face is falling falling you fucking cunt. You did that to me on purpose.

I didn't do shit, he said, you the one did the line just now when you know you got to be at work! How you gonna work now? How you gonna drive?

What is all your talk about coming through for yourself, showing up, flying right if you're gonna sabotage me like this?

You sabotaged yourself! Coulda waited till after work or done anything in the world with that. I asked you if you wanted it and you coulda said no! Don't blame this on me. You do gotta show up and fly right in your own life or you gonna lose everything.

This contorted exchange continued until Cal said Look I got to go, I got to get ready myself. You better get it together. You shouldn't be doin that stuff you don't know how to snap out.

Get the fuck out with your goddamned *I can be sober if I want cause I'm such a badass* voodoo! I said.

He left. I went into the kitchen and turned on a burner. I had slipped into such synesthesia that the clicking of the pilot made me have an orgasm. Propped on the back of the stove was a piece of broken mirror, a mirror I broke when I moved into that apartment. In the piece of mirror, which was shaped like Tennessee, my irises were gone. All-pupil looks vacant and deadly. And my movements had contrails as I looked away from the mirror and opened a drawer to find a steak knife. I heated the blade over the flame and then raised my cocktail dress—this was back when I still worked mostly in the bar at The Restaurant—and pulled down my pantyhose to get to my abdomen. I burned Cal's initials into the skin to the right of my navel, each about one inch square and made of straight lines, like letters carved into a tree. I felt and did not feel the pain. Skin melts like wax. I cut a big hole in the waist of the pantyhose so I could pull them back up and they wouldn't stick to the wound.

I don't know how I drove to work, all I remember is I had to sit down with Danny in the office and explain to him why I couldn't close my mouth or stop crying. I said something about my daughter. What I said was true, in the sense that it's true that that kind of coke will napalm your emotional synapses and whatever you care about most will suddenly be getting a sky's worth of air.

QUEER FUTURES

*Kehinde Bademosi, Zanele Muholi, and
Binyavanga Wainaina, with Shireen Hassim*

SHIREEN HASSIM: I wonder if you could address the way in which African publics are now more engaged with questions of sexuality. Does visibility marshal political power in ways that it didn't before? Have we dented the perception that only African elites can talk about sexualities? Does engaging publics through new media, through photography, through writing, change the political space? Binyavanga, let's start with you.

BINYAVANGA WAINAINA: Of course, Africa's a big and complicated continent...

I feel sometimes, as a gay person, like I'm sixteen years old, because it took me until my thirties to even engage with myself about my sexual identity—and now you go to these club balconies in Nairobi where queers have started to negotiate their own terms of engagement. There's one club in Nairobi which was fairly open, where a lot of classes mixed. At one point, the owner decided to ban gays. So gays boycotted the club, and it shut down. He came begging, but it shut down. In the club scene, the word must've gone around that banning gays is not good for business, and now we have balconies that are queer. The chemistries of younger generations are really fascinating in Nairobi.

About four years ago, a young man sent me a text message to say he was coming to my town. So we met. He told me, "Listen, I come from a village about fifty kilometers away from Eldoret, in an area that is known to be quite homophobic. I didn't even know that there was a thing called homosexuality, but I really liked fat men." He ended up in Eldoret, which is the nearest big town, and he went online, and found all the social media and web sites that many Africans know. The bright dig-

---

This transcript is adapted from a conversation that took place at the 2015 PEN World Voices Festival.

ital light helps people find their micro-communities in so many intense and specific ways, which maybe one can call coming out, or visibility.

HASSIM: It's interesting what you say about the bright light of visibility, which in some parts of Africa we've experienced as positively enabling, but in others, as in Uganda, the bright light of visibility and the public sphere of the law were used to regulate us in repressive ways. Zanele, you've worked to bring to awareness how having laws in place is not enough to protect people from hate crimes. I wonder if you could say something about your work and the work of photography around this visibilizing of sexualities in the public sphere.

ZANELE MUHOLI: Visibility can be risky for many people, especially in the townships where most South Africans grow up. Even in spaces where you think that you're protected the most, a lot of people have been hurt, and other people murdered. We took visibility to the streets of Johannesburg, Durban, and Cape Town—but I realized that was not the same for everybody.

Speaking of Africa, we're also speaking of visibility in terms of languages, because we can't just assume that visibility comes through English, as when our leaders say it's un-African to be queer because we don't have language for it. I'm speaking as a Zulu person and thinking of the number of languages that are spoken in our countries. We have eleven official languages in South Africa. How, then, do you make sure everybody understands without depending on academic terminologies that are mostly in English? How do we make sure that when you know for sure you're homosexual, you also have a sense of who you are, that it's okay for you to be Zulu, to be Xhosa, without modernizing your whole self and putting on a different kind of costume that will then make you foreign within your space? Can I be a Zulu female being and walk bare-breasted in public just like Zulu maidens, and reclaim my citizenship and my tribe?

We have to think in so many ways when we're thinking about what is visibility and what languages we use. I use visuals to write about our intimate spaces, to challenge the status quo. In South Africa, the internet is not as fast as here, and unlike most gay boys, we don't usually cruise. Maybe the format is easier for the guys because they know exactly what to do. We don't have any guidelines on how to make love to women, whereas boys just do it, you know. Gay bars are not my cup of tea, but they are relevant at the same time, because that's where people meet.

KEHINDE BADEMOSI: Okay, the digital media generation. I came to America a few months back, and I've been doing some research with gay men in Baltimore. I've been doing a lot of talking with them, especially the black men. I did a survey, and I found that out of 864 black men, only 12 percent of them would show their real photos on social media. Most of them are anonymous. Most of them want to hide themselves. Now, this is America, where there is protection for you if you are gay, but people are still hiding—because of what? There is a cultural element to this, and I think no matter what we do, even in the digital space, people are still going to respect culture. This is America, where there is a lot of freedom, but only 12 percent of black gay men would come online with their real pictures. Black gay men in America are still not visible. I think as we talk about Africa we should also reflect on what's happening here. Look at Black Lives Matter: I think there's a lot happening with black culture, and we need to contextualize this conversation. It's about the culture of shame and silence, these things that have brought us to this place where we are.

HASSIM: Right, and of course in large parts of this country, not only black queer people but white queer people don't feel safe, it seems. In Nigeria, do you think that there is more of an openness and a possibility of talking about sexualities in the public sphere?

BADEMOSI: Nigeria counts as the second most homophobic country in Africa, according to Pew research recently. In Africa, they surveyed about 45 countries, and Nigeria was second, with 90-something percent claiming that they don't want homosexuals. Remember that when the anti-gay bill was passed into law, in January 2014, the government said this was a Christmas gift to the nation, because people wanted to jail the gay people. Homosexuals in Nigeria are the sacrificial lambs for bad and corrupt governors. We are the ones that are the problem, not the terrorists, and not the people who are robbing the country blind. We are the ones who are the problem, because we are homosexuals. So anything that goes wrong… Like in America, even today they still say it is homosexuals when there's a hurricane, right?

HASSIM: Yeah, absolutely. And feminists.

BADEMOSI: Yes! So this is a universal thing. I used to talk about it as an African problem. When I moved here, I found out that this is a human problem. We try to hide behind the mask and blame other people for whatever predicaments we are facing.

HASSIM: Are the gay men in Baltimore feeling as if public spaces are spaces in which to be black is to be marked? So adding another layer to that, of an identity that is problematic, just reinforces their sense of vulnerability?

BADEMOSI: If you've been to Baltimore recently, you'll see most of the homes are boarded up, and it's 2015 in America. Many black people in the community don't have public transportation. We do not have public spaces like parks or places for children to play. There are issues already going on for these people; they don't want to add homosexuality to that. When you go to a typical barbershop—which is one of the places where I conducted my survey—you need to leave your homosexuality at the door. This is a black man's space, and as black men, we're listening to hip-hop, we're listening to rap music, and these artists fetishize the black male as tough and strong. Anything homosexual makes you look like you are losing the fight against the supremacist. So there are complex social problems, and I think the earlier we realize that, the easier we'll be able to leverage the right systems. This is not just Nigerian or Kenyan, you know. It is a universal problem.

HASSIM: One big problem in the postcolonial condition is the extent to which heterosexuality, and particularly the notion of a patriarchal family, remains so central. Zanele, your photography completely challenges the idea of the "virtuous female" of the nation, which is partly why the response is so violent, both the official response and the on-the-ground, in-the-street response to black queer women.

MUHOLI: You know, I try to do away with that word, "woman." I always use "female-bodied person," "being," "human being."

I think people are surprised when we take on the tools for production and produce work that then counts to history. I grew up in a space where only men carried cameras. When I realized that photography had no gender, I had to do it well, because if Binyavanga's face is on the wall, I've maybe shot that image the same way a guy would take those images, the same way a straight person or gay person could do the same. So I wanted to make sure that we had visuals that spoke to us, because I was tired of a lack of images that spoke to me as a person who is out and who is living as a black lesbian. I had to work, and I have to train other people to become photographers. What you had, or what you have, in your library at school was produced maybe twenty years ago, or thirty years ago. We need to produce the current that will speak to the future. Our productions, from videos to photographs, will always be different than the images produced in the '60s, '70s, and apartheid South Africa. Most of the work that's been produced of black people in Africa was never documented by us. We have a responsibility, as human beings, to claim our rights.

It's been twenty years of democracy now, and we have fewer books of our own than those that come from Kenya and other parts. There are people from outside who know more of South African queer history than us, which pains me. That's why I keep on echoing that need for the language, to say that if we use our own languages, we'll be moving in the right direction. Visibility basically means that people need to be able to read and write and visualize their daily experiences. Right now we don't have enough queer content that speaks to Africans in our own languages. I don't know why people think that we have to write in English. I'm a Zulu-speaking person. When you go to Zimbabwe, there are Shona people, there are Ndebele people, and if we were to use those languages, I think we'd be challenging our family members who think that we're adopting this concept from the West.

There's a need to write queer terms, terminologies, in our own vernacular. We say photography is universal, but my intentions with photography might not be the same as those of another queer person who comes from Kenya, or one who comes from Uganda. Even the art spaces curated by decent straight people—those curators are risking their jobs, because it means that the whole department has to have a long meeting just to negotiate whether you need to have black lesbian images with their naked selves there. It's a negotiation that is tiring, because you're thinking to yourself, *When will I ever be free?* The boys had Mapplethorpe, who produced amazing photography, where each time I look at those images—or when I look at Rotimi Fani-Kayode's work, I wish for two minutes to be a gay man for a day. As a lesbian, I have to think about showcasing images of black female bodies, with their boobs and their butts, in ways that I won't be termed the "controversial" black lesbian photographer. It has not been an easy journey.

HASSIM: Do you think Zanele is right, that it's easier for queer men than for women?

WAINAINA: I'm certain it's right. You have the double whammy of being a woman in the world and queer, and there's no way around all those structural challenges.

When Zanele and I spoke a while ago, about this idea of the archive, she said the state is weak in Africa because the state is fake. It's no secret. The invention of these countries was illegitimate. Now that they don't have a way to keep control (which was already tenuous) over people's activities, over people's imaginations, or over people's language, the state itself is imploding. Inside that implosion, there are all these opportunities to create small, possible utopias. That's why the idea of starting to build these archives is riper than ever, because people are ready for it, even without understanding.

At independence, people said, "I don't know what this is. I never contracted with a colonial master. That guy across my country on the other side, I didn't even know of his existence!" Then people went to school and were told, "That's your cousin from the map." So people said, "Okay, you can be my cousin, even though I really don't know you." Then we were told, "Put everything from home in a box, lock that box, and then come and perform Kenyan-ness, or Zimbabwean-ness." In the last fifteen years, people have begun asking questions about these identities, sometimes in extremely violent ways, in eruptive ways. In a certain sense, at the dead center, queers are asking. So I find myself in the cracks of a very beautiful moment, and for me, the front of the beauty becomes work like Zanele's. I mean, when I first encountered that work I thought, *It's not possible.* And it is. To make what five years ago I thought was physically impossible to do—and then when you go and look at the photographs you're like, oh, now that just looks normal. So cheers to you, Zanele.

BADEMOSI: What we're trying to say is: Let's change this language. Let's tell our stories. That's why Zanele's doing the heroic work of telling the stories of these women in the language of the people. Even black American people are not telling their stories. I'm in Baltimore, I'm trying to capture beautiful stories of black men who take their children to school, who play with their children. These stories are not told. What we hear is black men are criminals and all of that. I attended one of the top schools in America, and I realized that every time they sent us security warnings, they coded it like, "There are some black men that are moving around the campus...." I challenged the security and the school administration, and I said, "Why do you always put the color black in your e-mails to us?"

These are storytellers. Every letter, every magazine we see, every newspaper we see, these are all stories that are shaping us. These stories are being told over and over again—we need to change it. We need to let our people tell their own stories so we can change this language.

AUDIENCE: My question has to do with gender performance, identity, and authenticity. Does social media represent a new form of colonization, about how we're supposed to look no matter where we are within Africa? Are people taking on an image of homosexuality that they see abroad, or is it authentic to their own traditions?

BADEMOSI: If you look at mobile penetration in Africa, especially now that everybody has a mobile phone, you discover that there is a whole lot we can do with social media. I think it's a welcome thing, because now people are telling their own stories without being forced to listen to one single story, as Chimamanda Ngozi Adichie says about the danger of a single story. I think it's something we should celebrate, that digital social media is creating the space where we can have this new queer voice and identity and people have that space without being edited. With mobile phones in people's hands, they can talk about who they are, and they can pass it on. I think that's what causes revolution, even here in America. I think it's something we need to celebrate.

WAINANA: People have been living in Africa for two hundred thousand years as homo sapiens. Whatever the problems about the ownership of Twitter and which political party they belong to, and how Microsoft or Citibank shall try to own each and every person—at the same time you have Black Lives Matter. These platforms are not in and of themselves revolutions. But I am very, very interested in the idea of the power of the black person in this world. Where people are rushing and gushing through this to vault themselves into a place of power: yes.

AUDIENCE: In terms of making the lives of queers in Nigeria better, you have to engage religion. Is there a possibility of queer Nigerians and queer activists in Nigeria engaging with themes of Christianity?

BADEMOSI: I used to preach, and we had revival meetings—raising the dead, healing people. I can't tell you how many dead we raised, don't ask me! There are some activists in Nigeria who have pioneered the engagement with faith people. Jide Macaulay is someone I look up to. But if you look at our belief system, we are fanatical when we take anything on. We are intense. We need to engage religious leaders, but unfortunately these people are not going to just engage with us. I don't want to use the word "fanatics," but they will not listen to you. Jide Macaulay was persecuted, he had to flee. He was facing death threats because he was preaching and was using Jesus. In January this year, when I wrote my story about how I came out, I ended with the Book of Romans: "What shall separate us from the love of God?" That post went viral in Nigeria and most parts of Africa, and the reason people were fighting was not because I came out as gay, but because I quoted the Bible.

Religion was very destructive to me. I was with it, I was in it, I did everything. Then when I first came out, I would write anything against religion. Later on I realized we need to feel some empathy toward these people, so I started getting to be gentle. But people are still going to say, "You're going to hell because you are gay."

MUHOLI: We just want to change the systems in place. We all believe in love. We need to create those positive images that speak to us first, because we cannot rely on mainstream images that do not necessarily portray who we are. We cannot always rely on mainstream media deciding what should be on the covers of the magazines.

I'm producing from my community, and I'm not doing anybody a favor. This is about our lives, and we have a right to be seen in a positive way. We are at work, we want to change the history, we want to change the politics of how we are represented, we want to change how people look at us as we exist in different spaces. We use the same products, we pay the same taxes. When somebody collects our money they don't say "Don't collect the pink dollar, the pink ren," because it's the same money. When I produce, I hardly think of the mainstream. Instead what I do, I want to change how the mainstream looks at us. We want to change the literature, we want to change the history books, we want to change geographical areas that say queers can only be public once a year when there is Gay Pride. We are here 365 days of the year. Therefore, nobody is doing anybody a favor. We are working.

HASSIM: Binyavanga?

WAINAINA: I'm not saying anything just yet, she said it all!

HASSIM: She said it all, the sister said it all! The sister said it all.

ABOMINATION

Kehinde Bademosi

When Kehinde got off the bus in Lagos, he was weak from fasting but strong with the spirit of Sister Odolo, the Great Prophetess. The bus had dropped him off several blocks from his home on Market Street, where he lived with his twin sister, Taye, and his mother, Aduke, in a makeshift school. He had little more with him than a bag of Gala sausage rolls he'd bought along the way. It was after the New Year and most people had already left the city for the suburbs, where they celebrated the holiday with their families. Those who stayed had wrecked the city with parades and parties, leaving the streets littered with spent fireworks and the refuse of joyful celebrations.

Kehinde was eager to see Taye. He imagined that nothing dramatic had happened to her in the weeks he had been away. The doctors and psychiatrists had ensured that she would stabilize, but she still had occasional outbursts that were worrisome. Laura, his prayer partner from church, who had come to watch over Taye while he was gone, believed as Kehinde did that certain things were simply spiritual in nature, and only spiritual interventions could get rid of them. What afflicted Taye was a matter for prayer. Aduke was less certain, and her uncertainty tormented her. Was she to believe that her son, the newly anointed Preacher Boy, could bring home the miracle that would heal her daughter of her crippling psychosis? Or was she to have faith in the psychiatrist who claimed her daughter's illness was caused by a trauma of the "neural circuit"? No one knew exactly what that meant.

Laura believed in Kehinde. She was the one who knew Sister Odolo and had recommended that Kehinde visit her when the family's prayers for Taye went unanswered. Laura gave him comfort. Should anything happen at home while he was away, Laura knew how to reach him. People were always coming from and going to Ajebo campground for prayers, and if he was needed, all she had to do was send a note through one of the other believers.

It was easy to locate Kehinde at Ajebo campground. He was the scruffy Preacher Boy, the one who waited on Sister Odolo. Campers nicknamed him Elisha because they could call on him for special prayers whenever the Prophetess was unavailable. He learned quickly, and soon after arriving he was casting out demons. He had learned how to groan his prayers without actually speaking a word, a practice that was particular to Sister Odolo. And as he groaned he would hold his stomach with both hands and writhe back and forth and left and right in a rhythmic fashion he couldn't control. And then all at once, he would cry out a cacophony of phrases that no one could understand. This style of prayer was called "birthing." It was the prayer style of Sister Odolo that Kehinde had come to master. The indecipherable words he uttered startled sinners and made many confess their sins. Once, after Kehinde had led a session of prayer at Ajebo, a little girl confessed that during a meeting of witchcraft she had eaten two full-grown adults for dinner. Another man, visibly shaking under the influence of Kehinde's presence, related how he had been responsible for the misfortunes of his dying wife. When things got too heated during these revival meetings, Kehinde would call Sister Odolo to intervene. Whenever Sister Odolo arrived, there would be complete silence. Her eyes were sunk deep into large sockets on her oval face, and she didn't speak many words. Holding her stomach with her tiny hands, she would unleash a frenzied laughter that unsettled even the forest surrounding the campground. That was called laughing *in* the spirit. Kehinde had yet to master that when he left Ajebo.

Kehinde brought few possessions back from the camp. He had on the same plain gray shirt he had worn when he left Lagos. While at camp, he had washed the shirt and his underwear only twice, as Sister Odolo had barely given them time for such things. No serious gospel warrior would leave important activities like praying and fasting to wash his clothes. The Bible never recorded Jesus washing his clothes. Sister Odolo would say Jesus had no underwear to wash; all he had was a loincloth. *Seek ye first the Kingdom of God and all these things will be added unto thee.* Beauty. Grooming. Fashion. As far as Sister Odolo was concerned, these were frivolous activities that had led many believers to hell. In Kehinde's right hand was a big black King James Bible, rumpled at the edges, the pages packed with various bookmarks to get him quickly to the passages he needed.

The time was half past eleven, and most vendors along Oke Alfa had closed their stalls. The dirt road was bumpy and potholed and littered with empty cartons of sugar and empty tomato tins flattened out by the passing trucks that delivered goods to the market. Walking the short distance home, Kehinde was hungry and feeling weak and feeble from fasting. He tore open the wrapped sausage rolls and sank his teeth into the cold bread and the beef buried within.

As he approached Oke Koto, the last bend before his home on Market Street, he felt a strong force pulling at him. He was now on a busy road, where the night market sold everything. The last time he walked that route was with Laura on their way back from the church. She had told him about the street and the sin-filled redbrick building in the middle of all its busyness. She knew it well because she understood Hausa, the language spoken on Oke Koto.

The red building gave the street its life. People traveled from faraway states across Nigeria to trade there. They sold marijuana. They sold bets. They sold sex. The patrons of Oke Koto dressed piously to cover up the obvious nature of their trades, but Kehinde knew what was going on. Or he thought he knew. And what he thought he knew enraged him. He wanted to bring the Kingdom of God here. He needed to *birth* Oke Koto for God. He had been anointed by Sister Odolo, the Great Prophetess, to set the captives free, and Oke Koto might as well be the testing ground for his newly acquired spiritual authority.

Full of God's might, the Preacher Boy plunged into the crowd, making his way toward the redbrick building. Outside the entrance, a mallam grilled suya meat on the corner while a crowd of people waited in line for their orders. Kehinde entered the building, and the deeper he went, the dimmer it got. Faces were shades of dark gray, except for the occasional flicker of light from a cigarette lighter revealing hints of who they were. There were Alhajis in loose-fitting clothing negotiating in low tones with the prostitutes. Further in, he passed traders selling Fura de Nunu and Zobo, medicinal yogurts from northern Nigeria that men used to thicken their semen and enlarge the male organ. There were boys, too, barely twelve years old, selling cigarettes and weed rolled in old newspapers. The buyers were older men, sometimes in their thirties, sometimes in their seventies. These older men rarely wasted time. They would beckon the boy of their interest. They would price the weed in the rolled newspapers. They would pay, and then take the boy and disappear inside a locked room. When the boys returned, they were usually too tired to continue with their trade.

Kehinde's breath quickened. His body hummed as if it were in tune with what he was seeing, but his spirit felt violated. This enraged him. Sister Odolo had told him it was okay to be angry at sin. "Holy anger," she called it. Careful that no one was watching him, he slowly lifted his hand above his head and groaned his prayers until he was seized by the cacophony of unknowable language. He moved further into the red building. The Preacher Boy had come to Oke Koto on a mission.

Deep inside the building, Kehinde arrived at a large open space packed and throbbing with people. He stared incredulously; his eyes danced around in wonderment. Prostitutes lined the corridors, smacking gum, blowing bubbles, smoking cigarettes and weed, and some other things he couldn't quite figure out. He felt light-headed.

A well-dressed lady in full hijab smiled and flashed a golden tooth. He looked around, unsure if the smile was meant for him. She sashayed toward him. Laura had told him that the prostitutes in Oke Koto kept their bodies covered so as not to offend their Muslim patrons. The lady walking toward Kehinde had a pretty face and breasts that could not be contained or hidden by the hijab. They burst out in full rebellion. Without saying a word, she took the Preacher Boy by the hand and led him into her room, where she sat him on the floor on the only cushion. The air in the room was different—it smelled of lavender and citrus mixed with tobacco and weed.

"I am Aminat." She sat close to Kehinde. "What's your name, Al-haji?"

"Hussein." Kehinde gave the name his Muslim father called him before Kehinde went the way of the church.

"How much will you pay for two sweet ones?" Amina asked in a pleasant Hausa accent. Then she slowly opened her dress and released her breasts. She pulled Kehinde close and caressed his unkempt hair.

"JESUS!" Kehinde cried, holding his stomach with one hand and his Bible with the other. He had come to *birth* Oke Koto for the Kingdom of Christ and to set the captives free. More angry than startled, Aminat got up quickly, grabbed Kehinde by the arm, and pulled him toward the door. That's when Isiaku entered. Isiaku was tall, with thick hair and the chest of a boxer. He whispered something in Aminat's ear, and she left the room.

"The devil is using you all." Kehinde pointed his Bible at Isiaku.

"Ba turenshi," Isiaku said in Hausa, revealing his gold tooth.

"So you can't speak even a little English?"

"Ba turenshi," Isiaku repeated as he got very close to Kehinde and caressed his head as Aminat had. Kehinde felt something. He felt it in his bones and across his skin as Isiaku ran his hand across Kehinde's worn shirt to feel his chest. Kehinde's dick stiffened. He didn't like the way he felt, but he didn't fight it. He told himself he would confirm what Laura had told him about the red building: that men came here to have sex with other men. These men, the "dandaodus," as Laura called them in Hausa, had been a part of Hausa tradition until Muslims tried to suppress it. Some dandaodus behaved like women. They wore the local makeup and dresses and danced for other, more masculine men at their parties. During the day, they cooked for their men, who called them their wives. Isiaku was one of the masculine dandaodus. He was an abomination unto God.

Sister Odolo had said that homosexuality was one of the seven great abominations that would bring America to its knees and allow her to take control of the White House. Homosexuality, according to Sister Odolo, was God's way of giving people over to their reprobate minds because they refused to acknowledge and worship Him. Kehinde believed every word handed down from the Prophetess. Sister Odolo didn't say it was so; the Bible said it was so in the Book of Genesis. In the Book of Leviticus. In the Books of Timothy and Corinthians. And in the Book of Romans, where it was written: *Men abandoned the natural function of the woman and burned in their desire toward one another, men with men committing indecent acts and receiving in their own persons the due penalty of their error.*

However, something in his far past kept calling out to him. He had had a dream about it and remembered it now, with Isiaku before him.

When Kehinde was twelve years old, he had developed an indescribable fondness for his head teacher's son, Tunde Tuoyo. At fifteen, Tunde was the oldest boy in class, having repeated several grades due to his poor academic performance. Kehinde liked to stare at Tunde endlessly anytime they got together after school. Soon enough, Tunde began to stare back—the same fixed stare during which nothing was said. Tunde clearly enjoyed Kehinde's staring. One day after school, Tunde pushed Kehinde up against the wall, nailing his hands to the wall with his strong palms. Kehinde didn't resist. He closed his eyes as Tunde came closer until their foreheads rubbed against each other, then their noses. They seemed to breathe each other, and then their mouths connected as if they were chewing each other.

The Touyos relocated to Dubai, and everything about that kiss was supposed to have relocated with them. But Kehinde remembered every detail of it. The helplessness of it. The smell of onions on Tunde's breath.

That night in Oke Koto, as Isiaku pulled Kehinde closer, Kehinde breathed him in the way he had Tunde. Blood rushed in his veins. Isiaku gently took Kehinde's Bible and threw it in the corner. With his thick Hausa fingers he traced the outline of Kehinde's nipples, now visible under his shirt. Then, slowly as the lantern in the room dimmed, Isiaku thrust his lips on Kehinde's. Kehinde did not stop him. Perhaps he did not want to stop him. Like a lamb led to the slaughterer, he gave himself willingly to Isiaku.

Isiaku's hand moved further down along Kehinde's chest, and down to his abdomen. When his hand reached Kehinde's waist, he began to unfasten his belt buckle. Instead of spurning the invasion, Kehinde silently prayed that a higher spiritual power would win the battle that raged within and keep Isiaku from going any further. He prayed that he would stop enjoying the intimacy. He prayed that his dick would soften, and that his nipples would behave themselves. He prayed that Isiaku would stop.

Isiaku opened the clasp of Kehinde's belt and started to lower his head. In one cry, in the style of Sister Adolo, Kehinde *birthed* the spiritual strength that stopped Isiaku. The Kingdom of God suffered violence and violence would take it by force. Kehinde ran from Isiaku. He ran with all his strength out the door, down the crowded corridor, and out into the open street. The cool night air hit him hard. He walked hurriedly, hiding his face from everyone passing by.

Market Street had a curfew. Vigilantes assigned to close the rusty gates would be there any minute now. Kehinde walked fast, breathing in and remembering Isiaku as he made his way home. It wasn't garlic. It wasn't onions, either. What he tasted in the back of Isiaku's mouth lingered. Was it a weed concoction or a sedative of some sort? He recognized Isiaku's cologne though; he reeked of it. It was one of those locally brewed by the perfumers in the north, its smell too spicy and floral. Powerlessly, he carried the aroma all over his broken self the whole way home.

BETINA'S TAIL

Aurora Venturini
Translated by Roy Kesey

Betina has a psychic disorder

That was the psychologist's diagnosis. I don't know if I've got it right. My sister was afflicted with a twisted spinal column, and sitting down she looked like a hunchbacked bug with short little legs and amazing arms. The old lady who came to darn our socks thought that someone had hurt our mom during her pregnancies, the most horrific injury coming while she was carrying Betina.

I asked the psychologist what "psychic" meant. She answered that it was something that had to do with the soul, that I wouldn't be able to understand until I got older. But I figured out that the soul was like a white sheet inside the body, and when it got stained, that made you dimwitted like Betina, and a little like me.

As Betina wheeled herself in vroom-vrooming circles around the table, I noticed that dragging behind her was a little tail that stuck out through the opening in the back of the wheelchair, and I said to myself, That must be her soul slipping out of her.

I interrogated the psychologist once again, this time asking if the soul had anything to do with being alive, and she said it did, even added that when it went missing, that meant the person had died and the soul had gone to heaven if it had been good or to hell if it had been bad.

Vroom, vroom, vroom. Betina kept dragging her soul around, and I noticed that each day it got a little longer, had a few more gray stains, and I deduced that pretty soon it would fall off and Betina would die. But I didn't care because she made me sick.

Roy Kesey was awarded a 2015 PEN/Heim Translation Grant for his translation of *The Cousins* by Aurora Venturini.

Whenever mealtime arrived, I had to feed my sister, and I would pick the wrong orifice on purpose, poke the spoon in her eye, her ear, her nose, before arriving at her big fat mouth. The miserable wretch would moan and moan.

I would grab her by the hair and push her face into her bowl and finally she'd shut up. Why should I be blamed for my parents' mistakes. I considered stepping on the tail that was her soul. The story about hell stopped me.

During communion I always read the catechism and "Thou Shalt Not Kill" had been burned right into me. But a poke here, a poke there, and the tail no one else could see kept growing. I was the only one who saw it and it brought me joy.

Institutes for special students

I wheeled Betina to her institute. Then I walked to the one where I was enrolled. At Betina's they dealt with the grimmest cases. The pig-boy, blubber-lipped, big fat face and little pig ears, he ate off a plate of gold and drank his broth from a golden bowl. He grabbed the bowl with his fat little ungulate hooves, and slurped with the sound of water pouring down into a well; when he ate solid foods, his jaws and his ears both moved, and he couldn't quite bite down with the tusks that stuck out like those of a wild boar. One time he looked at me. His tiny eyes, two inexpressive little marbles, hidden in all that fat, stayed on me. I stuck out my tongue and he grunted and threw his tray on the floor. The caregivers came and had to calm him down by tying him up like an animal, which is exactly what he was.

While I waited for Betina's class to end, I walked up and down the din-filled hallways. I saw a priest accompanied by an acolyte. Someone had handed in their sheet, their soul.

The priest said, If you have a soul, may God take it to his bosom.

To whom or what had he said it?

I went closer, and saw that he was with a prominent couple from Adrogué. On the table was a cannelloni sitting on a silk cloth. Except it wasn't a cannelloni, it was something expelled from a human womb, otherwise the priest wouldn't be baptizing it.

I asked around, and a nurse told me that every year this distinguished couple brought in a cannelloni to be baptized. That the doctor had advised them to stop procreating because there was no cure for the wife's condition. And that they'd said they couldn't stop on account of being extremely Catholic. Even with my disability I knew how disgusting the whole thing was, but I couldn't say that to the nurse. That night I was so repulsed I couldn't even eat.

And my sister's soul kept growing.

Developing

Betina was eleven and I was twelve. Rufina said, You're at the age where you start developing. I thought something would emerge from inside of me and I prayed to sweet Saint Theresa that it wouldn't be a cannelloni. I asked the psychologist what "developing" meant and she went red and suggested I ask my mom.

My mom also went red, and said that at a certain age girls stopped being girls and became young ladies. After that she fell quiet, leaving me in suspense.

As I've said, I was attending an institute for people who were disabled but not as disabled as Betina. A girl there said she'd already developed. I didn't see anything different. She told me that when it happens, your crotch bleeds for several days and you shouldn't take a bath and you need to use a rag to keep from staining your clothes and you have to be careful with boys because you can end up pregnant.

That night I couldn't sleep, and I felt around the area in question. It wasn't moist, so I could still talk to boys. When I developed, I wouldn't go anywhere near them, to keep from getting pregnant and having a cannelloni or anything like that.

Betina talked a lot, or mumbled in a way you could understand. One night during a family gathering that she and I weren't allowed to attend because of our lack of manners, especially at the table, she shouted in a voice like a trombone, "Mom, my pussy's bleeding!" We were in the room right next to where the banquet was happening.

A grandmother and two cousins came in.

I told the cousins not to go anywhere near the bleeding because they could end up pregnant. Everyone got offended and left and Mom hit us both with her pointer.

I went to my institute and told everyone that Betina had developed in spite of being a year younger than me. The teacher lectured me about how we shouldn't say such immoral things in the classroom, and gave me an F in Civic and Moral Education. Instead of being a class we were now a bunch of worried students, especially the girls, who were touching themselves every so often to check for possible moistness.

Just to be sure, I never hung out with boys again.

One afternoon Margarita came in glowing. She said, I got it, and we all knew what that was about.

My sister left school in the third grade. That was as far as she could go. Actually, neither of us was going far, and I left in the sixth grade. Yes, I learned to read, and to write but with spelling mistakes, especially words with a silent *h*—if it isn't pronounced, what's it good for?

I was reading dyslalically, is what the psychologist said. She suggested that I'd get better with practice, and she made me recite tongue-twisters like, If two witches were watching two watches, which witch would watch which watch?

Mom watched, and when I couldn't untwist the sentence she smacked me in the head with her pointer. The psychologist banned her from the room during tongue-twisters and I started untwisting better, because when Mom was there I tried to finish the witches quickly, but I was so afraid of getting smacked with the pointer that I made mistakes.

Betina rolled vrooming around us, opened her mouth, and pointed inside because she was hungry.

I didn't like eating at the table with Betina. She made me sick. She drank her soup straight out of the bowl without even using a spoon, and grabbed solid foods with her hands and wolfed them down. She cried if I insisted on sticking the spoon in every orifice in her face.

They bought Betina a feeding chair that had a little table attached to it, and a hole in the seat so that she could defecate and pee. Halfway through meals she would always feel the need. The smell made me vomit. Mom said not to pretend I was some delicate flower or she'd lock me up in the nuthouse. I knew all about the nuthouse, and from then on I ate, shall we say, perfumed with the stink of my sister's poop and raining piss. When she farted, I pinched her.

After eating, I went out in the yard.

Rufina sanitized Betina and sat her in her wheelchair. The dope napped with her head down on her bosom, or actually on her bosoms, because her clothes now revealed two nice round provocative bulges because she'd developed before me, so even though she was gross she became a young lady before I did, which meant Rufina had to change Betina's rag every month and wash her crotch.

I made do on my own, and observed that my little boobies weren't growing, that I was still thin as a broomstick, or Mom's pointer. Our birthdays came and went year after year, but I started drawing and painting classes at the Fine Arts High School, and the art teacher said that I'd become an important artist because thanks to being half crazy I could draw and paint just like the most notorious artists of recent times.

The exhibition at Fine Arts

The professor said to me, Yuna—that's what everyone calls me—your artwork is worthy of being included in an exhibition. Some of it just might even sell.

I was so overwhelmed with happiness that I jumped on top of him with my whole body and stayed clinging to him with all four of my limbs, my arms and legs, and we fell down together.

The professor said that I was very pretty, and that when I grew up we'd start dating and he would teach me things as beautiful as drawing or painting but that I shouldn't tell anyone the news of our project, which in reality was all his idea, and I imagined that it would involve bigger and bigger exhibitions and I jumped on him again and kissed him. And he kissed me back, blue-tinted kisses that had repercussions in places I won't name because that would be wrong and then I found a big canvas and without sketching anything first I painted two red mouths pressed together, interlocked, united, inseparable, song-filled, and two eyes above, blue, the kind out of which slip crystal tears. The professor, on his knees, kissed the painting and there he stayed, in the shadows, and I went home.

I told Mom about the exhibition; not knowing anything about art, she answered that my shapeless monstrosities would make all the other Fine Arts students laugh, but if that's what the professor wanted, it didn't make any difference whatsoever to her.

At the exhibition my work was up alongside the work of other students, and two of my pieces sold. Too bad that one of them was the one with the kisses. The professor had baptized it "Primer Amor." That seemed fine to me. But I didn't completely understand the meaning.

Yuna has promise, said the professor, and I liked that so much that every time he said it I stayed after class to jump on him. He never scolded me for it. But when my boobies started to grow, he said that I had to quit, because man is fire and woman straw. I didn't understand. But I didn't jump on him anymore.

The diploma

So I graduated from Fine Arts when I was seventeen, but because of my dyslalia I would never be able to teach there, or even give private lessons. All the same I painted whenever I could afford the paper, and the professor, who often came to visit us, gave me paints.

Betina rolled her vroom chair in circles around the professor until he got dizzy, but Mom would never let the two of us be alone together and once she slapped me maybe because she saw us kissing each other even though it was just on the cheek, not on the mouth the way movie actors do.

I was always afraid she wouldn't let the professor come inside. But she always did as long as we hadn't been kissing each other, because if the devil sticks in his tail and the professor sticks in a certain part of his masculine anatomy I could get pregnant and the professor would never marry a disabled student.

Betina rolled in more circles than ever when the professor came to give me private lessons and look at the paintings and drawings that were piling up against the wall with a view toward an exhibition in Buenos Aires.

One time, night fell and Mom invited the professor to stay for dinner and he accepted. I was shaking at the thought of the disgusting sounds, rains, and smells that came from Betina's carcass. But when the captain's aboard, a sailor has no sway.

Rufina had made cannelloni, which on top of everything else made me remember the madhouse cannelloni. I suddenly wanted to paint in order to burn off some energy. I painted something that only I could understand: a cannelloni with eyes, and above it a hand that was giving it a blessing. In my mind I whispered, If you have a soul, may God take it to his bosom.

WORD PROBLEMS

TC Tolbert

5. On Monday, X ate a banana with peanut butter for breakfast, a Clif bar for lunch, and 4 pieces of fudge and 2 Reese's for dinner. On Tuesday, X hiked 10 miles and ate Greek yogurt with fresh fruit, cashews, an apple, a Clif bar, and pasta. On Wednesday, X started the day with red velvet cake. If food addiction is twice as likely in women who experienced physical or sexual abuse before 18, is X a woman or a man?

7. There are only two kinds of bodies: living and non-living. If X notices the still-wet grass underneath the car, wants to brush it with a cheek, imagines not a place to hide but a space to be pressed (pulled?) across nature and machine, who killed/didn't kill X?

8. This section has multiple parts.

X is building a body in the shape of a body. Silence is as dependable as conversation. Though the body's shape will no longer be southern, X's body in the shape of a body will always be from the south.
Question 1: Who is/isn't afraid of the shape of a body (aka a "shadow")?
Question 2: Who says the most—the body in the shape of a body or the hole in the shape of a mouth?

Given that X is white, X's body in the shape of a body will also be white. All the men in X's family own guns.
Question 3: What is the relationship between fear, race, and resources?
Question 4: Who is running?
Question 5: Why?
Question 6: What does it mean to "finish first"?
Question 7: When will white men's bodies feel safe at home?

X's body in the shape of a body is currently living in a car. The car is white and has traversed the country twice in three months. This is a choice. X's body in the shape of a body has masturbated at high speeds, shopped at gas stations late at night, and slept comfortably while parked on the side of the road. X doesn't understand this word—freedom—but prays it has nothing to do with camouflage.

Question 8: What is it that turns X's body in the shape of a body into a ghost?

BLESSED BODIES

Dorothy Tse

Translated by Nicky Harman

Y-land had no marriage system but was famous for its prosperous sex industry. Even bartering was allowed: When the male clients could not afford to pay, they could obtain sexual services by trading their body parts. At the moment of sexual arousal, a man would stand in the doorway, peeping into a dim room where a woman reclined on the bed. Once she adopted the desired position, he no longer cared about his arms or legs. But with the ebbing of arousal, the man would open his eyes to see what had once been his limb—first amputated, then frozen, bottled, and removed. Only then would he be astonished at the impulsive decision he had made.

Amputees could be seen all over Y-land, hobbling heroically along the city streets. The limbs that had once belonged to them were stored in special depots. There, glass bottles of all sizes were arrayed on rusty iron shelves in packed rows. The refracted light made the limbs, floating in preserving fluid, appear grossly deformed. Soon they would be loaded onto ships and sold to the developed countries that bordered Y-land.

At times of peak arousal, the impoverished men of Y-land milled around in the streets, gazing up at the dead leaves that floated from the trees or down at their own big feet. In the sunshine, they were accompanied by anxious shadows that crept along behind them, looming over the bodies to which they were attached.

In October, the girl and her brother arrived in Y-land by boat. The streets were full of people selling creamlettes. They ladled golden batter onto sizzling hotplates, where it spread out and set in perfect disks that seemed to hint at a blessed life.

"You'll lose your body here," said her brother as he bought her a creamlette.

The cream oozed out over the thin greaseproof paper and onto her brother's hand—like happiness brimming over. But the fragrance of the creamlette just made her want to vomit.

A doctor, sitting across the rectangular white table from them, reassured her, "Being sick has nothing to do with pregnancy. You're only feeling seasick because you've imagined your room as a boat."

They took the girl and her brother up to the top floor of an old building. It was just as she had imagined it, so dark green it seemed to have moldered to the point of disintegrating.

In this gloomy apartment there were two rooms, each with gray walls and an oversized bed. It took the girl some time to locate the tiny window, high up on the wall and pasted shut with newspaper that had yellowed with age. She stood on tiptoe on the bed, pushed the window open, and saw the mist from the street rippling toward her.

The girl really did believe from the start that this building was a boat. The first time she stepped on the floor, it felt insubstantial. The sound of waves reached her from outside the window, and the floor seeped water, so that the girl, alone with the few sticks of furniture, became frantic at the thought of going moldy.

In the middle of the night, the girl always felt terrified that the boat was spinning on the crest of a wave. The floor seemed to be bucking and rearing, and she would stagger into the other room, crawl into her brother's bed, and sleep with him. When she woke up the next morning, she would rush to the window and look out, to reassure herself that she had not been carried off to another unknown place.

The girl liked the narrow street outside the building. Sometimes, the street was enlivened by men passing by, brandishing knives or glass jars, especially when their rich red blood dyed the asphalt and the trash heaped on it. Her eye was often caught by a bloodstained plastic bag fluttering in the breeze.

It did not take her brother long to discover that she had brought in sacks filled with stones. These she placed individually in each corner. But nothing stopped her feeling queasy, and she was forced to take the seasick pills the doctor had prescribed.

In November, the girl placed her feet side by side, joining her big toes together. It was cold, as cold as the yellow glass on the opposite side of the street. Behind the glass, she could see the face of a young man, tilted slightly upward. The young man's gaze was climbing right into her window. The face appeared so often that she came to regard it as part of the street scene.

Her brother was surprised when she said she wanted to go outside and put up leaflets to sell herself.

She had head lice. He made her sit on a stool and he carefully separated the strands of her hair, combing out the gray-black eggs with a fine-toothed comb so that they plopped onto a metal tray. He had to crack the really stubborn ones between his fingernails before he could pull them out.

"They said you could wait six months," said her brother, dousing her head with kerosene and wrapping it in a towel. There was a powerful stink in the air.

The girl paid no attention. She just smiled. Her face was covered in dimples, so that when she smiled, it always looked as if she was crying.

The girl told them she wanted a huge mirror so that she could see her whole body. It should be smooth and shimmering and reflect her in the minutest detail. When she washed her hair, she would sit in front of the mirror and coil it up. Then she would strip naked and look at her budding figure. She was so skinny that her bone structure was clearly visible under the skin. Under her right breast, there was one abnormally sunken rib.

"What do you think?"

Her brother was standing by her bed, looking out the window at the scenery. "Too pale, too thin."

"How about these?" asked the girl, indicating the slight protuberances of her breasts.

"Them, too."

But the girl realized her brother was not looking at her properly, so, paying no attention to what he thought, she dressed again, grabbed a sheaf of leaflets, and ran downstairs. All down the stairwell, the walls were completely covered with black leaflets, and there were more in the noodle shop at the bottom of the stairs. The people slurping their noodles and looking through the window, at a world made dark by the leaflets, thought it was the end of the world. No matter, the sorrow they felt sharpened their appetites and the hot noodles made them a little tipsy. The steam from their bowls obscured their coarse features and, in their excitement, men and women began to play footsie under the tables.

The young man came over to the girl. He was dressed in a baggy black sweater, and his hair was cropped short. The girl had not realized until then just how pallid he was, almost like someone in a black-and-white photograph. He tore down one of her leaflets, and a single patch of red appeared on each pale cheek. It was, thought the girl, as rich a color as the bloodied plastic bags that she had seen in the street.

The mother, seeing her one-armed son standing in the doorway, was not surprised. It was as she had foreseen. The night sky was not very dark. There was a row of four streetlamps, but only one of them emitted a flickering light, and her son stood under it in his black sweater. His empty left sleeve dangled limply, showing that now he was a man. He had grown tall and slender, and looked as desolate as an empty road.

His amputation did not worry his mother. All the men in Y-land learned to do everything one-handed from boyhood, even buttoning their coats with both feet, as well as all sorts of other minor tasks. What did worry her was the way he lay in bed biting his fingernails and smiling a little smile. He just looked too blessed. It seemed that he didn't regret the loss of an arm at all.

Silently, in a funereal mood, his mother got his dinner ready. Her son carried on lying on the bed: his head to one side, his eyes shut, day after day, in the same position. His mother was mostly puzzled by this, although sometimes the scene filled her with an almost religious fervor.

Hordes of ants began to gather at his bedside, as if on a pilgrimage. His mother took a broom and, as she swept, heaps of Coca-Cola cans clattered out from under the bed. She remembered how, years before, he used to lie in bed, obsessed by books on witchcraft. He ate nothing as he read; he just drank Coke. He kept this up for four years. After his mother washed the old Coke cans, she covered the walls of the house with them, and used them to erect a fence outside the house too. The dazzling red of the cans filled her with a near certainty that he would risk his life for his obsession.

Once when she was sure that her son was asleep, she located the ten cans in the Coke wall that she had marked and stuffed with twenty-dollar bills, and skillfully extracted them. After she checked to make sure that none of the money was missing, she hesitated for a very long time, thinking about whether to use the money to fulfill her son's desires, but finally decided against it. Before putting the cans back in place, she took a roll of bills from one of them and put it under the seventh floorboard from the door, the one right next to the wall.

The money would be enough to give her son a decent funeral, she thought to herself.

The young man was dreaming of a vast ocean. At first it was not an ocean, but a huge bed. The naked girl was at one end of the bed, sitting cross-legged. Above her knees, he could see a pair of flat breasts that looked like oversized eyes. But the eyes were not looking at him. They gazed at a boat far, far in the distance.

The girl told him that before he came along, she often felt she was being bowled over and over in the sea, all alone, being blown by the wind to a place she did not recognize. So every time she got out of bed, she thought she had landed on a strange new shore.

"After you came along, I felt that we were trying madly to reach the shore together, but just as we were almost there, you would turn and leave me."

The girl's words hurt the young man. He began to weep, his tears salty like seawater. His sorrow turned blue and shrouded the whole dream. This persuaded him that the ocean was huge.

When the young man woke up, he told his dream to a man in a black jacket who happened to be passing by outside the front door. "This must be what they call love, mustn't it?" the man responded in a low voice.

He did not know the man, but he ended up inviting him into the house. As a result, the man became his mother's client, and so lost an eye.

The girl had few visitors, and those that did come hardly ever came back for another visit. The girl had nothing to do. She stood on the bed with her brother, looking out the tiny window into the narrow alley outside. Occasionally there were passersby, and the girl made her brother guess whether they would come upstairs.

By now the weather was getting warmer; people were wearing clothes that were too tight and made them puff and pant. Two men stood down below, looking up at the girl's window. They stood there a long time.

"They won't come," her brother said, as he always did.

The girl was indignant. She stuck her head out of the window and waved energetically, but the men below lowered their heads and hurried away.

Her brother could not help smiling.

He had not told the girl how he detested her shutting the apartment door and making him wait outside. When that happened, he fidgeted anxiously, then got out his pen and wrote random hieroglyphics all over the gray wall. On and on he wrote, until his hand and arm ached.

When the visitor finally left, the girl liked to go up to the wall, connect the hieroglyphics, and make them into a song. She would sing out hoarsely: hua-hua-you-dad-tu-tu...la-la...sha-bu-dong-me-he-ya...

She made the tune sound quite festive, and could keep it up until evening. Her brother particularly disliked having visitors in the evening because, if no one came, the girl would put her arms around his neck, bury her head in his armpit, and fall fast asleep. When she woke up again, she would tell him all the dreams she'd had.

Just at that moment, someone else came into view down in the street. It was the young man, now one-eyed, walking with the aid of a stick, tapping his way along with a cheerful rhythm.

Of all the visitors, her brother disliked the young man most, because when he and the girl shut the door on him it always felt like a century before they opened it up again.

Y-land folk all knew that the young man had already lost an arm and a leg and an eye for the girl. "You should hang on to your hand," the girl told him, "to stroke my face, my thigh, and my ribs... What else can you give them?"

"It's my liver this time," said the young man, with a slight smile, his pale face flushing once more.

The girl was reassured and smiled. Everyone said that when the girl smiled, it always looked as if she was crying.

The girl dreamed she was sitting in a boat, sailing to a small island. But it was too dark on the island, and the girl could not be sure that was what it was.

Then she saw a light, perhaps from a streetlamp in the center of the island. She felt her way toward the source of the light, only to find that it was not a streetlamp but the young man standing there. By now he had lost both arms, and was left with just one leg to hold his body upright. It was his right eye that was emitting the light. She had not realized it was so bright. It was a pity that the eye was so high up; she could not reach it, even on tiptoe. Otherwise, she could have dug it out and patrolled the island, holding it in her cupped hands. The young man's remaining leg had sunk deep in the ground by now and the girl sat down, leaning against his leg, until the light disappeared.

When she woke up, she told the dream to her brother. He said nothing, just gently wiped the sweat from her body. His hand slid from her flat chest, down over the sunken rib. Then it stopped, and he kissed her.

A light spread out in all directions, and it was possible to make out things that were represented by a variety of colors. The pink seemed to be dust, the green was mold, the violet was a puff of hypnotic powder, and the yellow was aged light. Finally, everything faded from view.

Such was the scene the young man saw before he lost his second eye. When everything had gone pitch-black, and the blackness had no trace of color left in it, he discovered he was in terrible pain. He begged to be taken home. After all, he was an old customer.

They told him they were putting him into a wooden cart, but it felt to him like he was being tossed head over heels like a fish in a huge frying pan, until every one of his still-unhealed wounds burst open. He could not tell whether what he was feeling was scorching heat or pain.

They laughed at him. "That's because Y-land's roads are full of potholes," they said, "and have wrecked cars, dead fish, and bottles of lubricating oil piled up on them."

As they went along, they took turns describing the scenery to the young man so he could tell them the way. There was an abortion clinic on the corner, they said, the one run by the woman doctor, Dr. Tang, with the gleaming white skin and great fat fingers. There was a stall selling placenta next door to the clinic, but most of the placenta was fake, just something made from gelatin. He said he did not remember the clinic or the shop. He probably had not come this way before.

"Then you can't have been inside Y-land's first cinema, right? They show all sorts of porn films there."

This made them all feel sorry for the newly blind young man. By this time, they had given up asking him how to get back to his home, and were just taking him wherever they felt like, singing at the top of their voices: hua-hua-you-dad-tu-tu...la-la...sha-bu-dong-me-he-ya...

Meanwhile, the young man's mother had gotten his dinner ready and had been sitting waiting for him for a long time. Her eyelids felt so heavy, and even though she heard the distant sound of singing, her head dropped on the table and she fell fast asleep.

The young man did not know what time it was—probably morning, to judge by the slight warmth of the sun that fell on his face. Now he had a new way to experience the sun.

"It's so dark," he said.

The girl did not know if the young man ever visited again, because soon afterward, she left Y-land.

On her brother's bed, she discovered a wad of cash. "They want you to get rid of the child," said her brother.

But his mouth was full of toothpaste and the girl could not understand what he was saying.

When he finished brushing his teeth and went back into the room to find her, the girl was gone, wandering aimlessly and alone through the dawn streets. On the pavement, there was a one-eyed old man making stuffed creamlettes with golden-yellow cream, too much of it. The girl bought one. It was the first time she had tasted one of these golden creamlettes. Its sweetness startled her, as did the fact that she liked it very much.

The street cleaner was washing down the pavement with detergent. The girl sat on a bench, nibbling carefully at the creamlette until it was all gone. By the time she had finished, bubbles were rising up from the street into the air, sailing toward some nearby railings in the morning sunlight, and then bursting, perhaps because the sun was too bright. Beyond the railings, countless silent boats were moored.

The girl finally bought herself a boat ticket to an unknown destination. When she stepped on deck, it felt curiously stable. She would not have known they were moving but for the ship's horn. After she got pregnant, she did not vomit anymore. Her body felt heavier and heavier, and even standing on deck she did not feel like she was floating.

It was night and the boat passengers had gone to sleep. The girl discovered the cabin was full of doors, all with bolts. She tried to open them and realized they were not real bolts at all. There was nothing behind most of the doors, just an enormous hold which seemed bigger even than the entire boat. Behind one, however, was a room filled with bottles of yellow liquid. Each bottle was marked with a time and date. The largest bottles were filled with very long legs; the smallest held eyeballs. The girl crouched down and found a bottle labeled "2002-7-28 19:30," with a small, bright eyeball in it. She picked it up and put it in her pocket. Once, she remembered, this eye had been embedded in the young man's face.

She realized that there was one woman on the boat who was not asleep. The woman's son had died a week before. The woman had sold as many of her son's body parts as she could, so she did not have to pay a cent for the funeral. The mother, old and faded-looking, had decided to leave Y-land after it was over. Before she left, she strung together some of the Coke cans she had stored in her son's room and attached them to her only long skirt. Now she was on the boat, and the clanking of the cans, with their glittering red color, was her way of grieving for her son.

from **ON PARADISE**

Roger Reeves

I was born big enough to bear several disasters.
Now, my body hangs in a tree like a bridge
You once stood upon to watch a city disappear
Into fog and fire. "Your mumbling will drive centuries,"
Said my grandmother who also warned me
I would have to lose my tongue in order to gain
Speech. Speak. Open fire, open fire. Who grew
Tired of my tongue and toes and left me here
With an incomplete utterance about Paradise?
These blind bird heads bouncing in the wind augur
Answers to every question of troubled flight
But my last. When asked to speak with angels,
I spoke. When I was a bowl, I was a bowl.
Or my tongue. Or the river. When I drove
This body to its river sequestered within
Its banks, the body asked nothing of my driving.
When a snake at the bottom of the Mississippi
Bit my tongue, I stuffed straw from the road
Into my mouth. And when I heard voices fretting
In the figs, in the maple, in the mouth of a panther,
I followed them out into whatever fire, creek,
Or congress of bats littered the attic walls.
"Ain't your fault God gave you so much
Black. Appetite." she said. "Ain't your fault
Black is the color that lights the grave
And its appetite." Who will forgive the Good Lord
For this error of love and fame and famine,
For the bears and bobcat-paw-police my whistling

Called out of the wilderness, the birds falling
Dead behind me. Master of Beauty and the Blood-
Moon, I did what you told me to do: underground
Underground, underground your sorrows,
The afterbirth blackening into absence. I am
Weary of living this far into my death, tired
Of the sound that runs of my bones, (was)
Almost content to be a wound. But I was born
Dark and mumbling in this buried room.

•

Though I have the groin of an angel—light,
Castrated, holy and missing—not so much a missing
But a there that is not there, less the charity
Of pleasure—the capacity to pierce, sunder, or run,
Which any common mule will do—whipped or not whipped—
Because, after all, running is the last attempt at rescue.

•

And the running was less the whip and more
What the whip signaled—a going down and a coming
Up, a back and forth between all knowledges and none,
Of which the dead though granted access, do not always partake
Finally aware that the speaking could only occur after death,
When nothing needs explanation and the heart finally refuses and
    accepts the body.

•

You want a story, but you already have one:
I went up and came down. Simple as a ditch.
When a ram lies down in dew, he rises wet
Between the legs. When a man falls from a woman
Bucking and crying like a stag caught in a barbwire fence,
My God, he's nothing more than a singing grave.

•

Can't no grave hold my body down...
No matter what I do I cannot escape
My dead children. How they lurch out of my hair,
Walk out the ocean and lie across my lawn.
Even the rabbits savaging the carrots and chrysanthemums
Avoid my children's discarded chains and limbs in the light
    hum of the grass.

                        •

Now that I am dead, I can finally smell spring
Even in the rust of October when the hay in the barn settles
Its perfume into anybody or evening or sky
Or turtle carried off into the red burst of a field
Limp in the jaws of a dog. Yes, that's spring all right—
Ruinous, smiling, taking our bodies up.

                        •

There is no narrative to my seeing though there is a nation
        Below me. The wild hogs carry me
  Between their hooked teeth and grunting song.
                And when they tire of my passing meat, they eat.
        Sometimes, if I'm not careful, I speak
                    As both hog and disappearing man
            As I do now, as I do often. I am
    But one animal
            Framed inside of another.
                        When I was a man, I spoke as a man.
                But when I became a pig, I found no need
                    To speak though I can tell you of hunger
                And eating your own brother
                            Because he was red
And cast before you, the gnats riding their own small bulbs of hunger
    Toward his decaying door, gnawing where I had not.
                        And were I to let this meat rot
                You would ask what type of animal am I?
            I, too, have waited until no one looked

And gorged on what was left.
I, too, have been left hungry
And drifted into an orchard and ate
Apples that caused me to retch up
What was perfect flesh
Hours before. My guts, thorn and briar—my body held as if in a thicket.
As if hostage and answer for some god
To send along a father
Who's meant to slay his son by the throat. Yes, I'd rather eat
My brother than become the animal
Crazed in the vines awaiting the stone table and blade
Of one nation
To fall upon my neck and forget my name. Swine.

SURVIVING THE WRECK

Tom Stoppard

By misfortune, they had struck the reef at high tide, and as the seas grew violent, attempts to free the ship failed. The frigate was assuredly lost: It was decided to build a raft. A raft was made, and well made. One hundred and fifty was to be the complement of the raft. Those onboard had wine, a little brandy, some water, and a small portion of sodden biscuit. They had been given no compass or chart. With neither oars nor rudder, there was no means of controlling the raft.

In the first night, a storm got up and threw the machine about with great violence. By daybreak, the air was filled with cries, and all prepared themselves for death. The next day, the seas were calm, and for many, hope was rekindled. It was during this day that those on the raft began to experience their first delusions. Some fancied that they saw land, others thought they espied vessels coming to save them.

The second night was more terrible than the first. A group of men, certain that they were lost, broke open a cask of wine to soothe their last moments by abandoning the power of reason, in which they succeeded, until the seawater spilled and spoiled the wine. Thus doubly maddened, these disordered men determined to send all to the common destruction, and to this end attacked the ropes that bound the raft together. The mutineers being resisted, a pitched battle took place among the waves and the darkness of the night before order was restored. But at midnight, the soldiery rose again, and attacked their superiors with knives and sabers. Men were thrown in the sea, bludgeoned, stabbed. Two barrels of wine were thrown overboard and the last of the water. By the time the villains were subdued, the raft was laden with corpses.

The third day was calm and fine. They took repose, but cruel dreams added to the horrors already inflicted by hunger and thirst. The raft now carried less than half of its original complement.

This transcript is adapted from remarks presented at Opening Night of the 2015 PEN World Voices Festival.

On the fourth morning, they perceived that a dozen of their fellows had died in the night. The bodies were given to the sea, except for one, that was reserved against their hunger. It was from this day onwards that all learned to consume human flesh. The next night was to bring a fresh supply: Once more, a terrible combat ensued and blood washed over the fatal raft. There remained no more than thirty onboard. Barely a man lay without wounds into which salt water constantly flowed and piercing cries were heard.

On the seventh day, two soldiers concealed themselves behind the last barrel of wine. They struck a hole in it, and began to drink. On being discovered, they were thrown and cast into the water. Now the most terrible decision had to be taken. On counting their numbers, it was found that they were twenty-seven. Fifteen of these were likely to live for some days. The rest, suffering from large wounds, and many of them delirious, had but the smallest chance of survival. After a debate in which the most dreadful despair presided, it was agreed among the fifteen healthy persons that their sick comrades must, for the common good of those who might yet survive, be cast into the sea.

After this cruel sacrifice, the last fifteen survivors threw all their arms into the water, reserving only a saber, lest some rope or wood need cutting. Under the burning sun, a raging thirst consumed them, until they began to moisten their lips with their own urine. Sharks now surrounded the raft, and some soldiers, in their derangement, openly bathed within sight of the great fish.

On the thirteenth day, the sun arose entirely free from clouds. The fifteen wretches had put up their prayers to the Almighty, and divided amongst them the portion of wine, when a captain of infantry, looking towards the horizon, descried a ship. An offering made thanks to the Lord. They straightened barrel hoops and attached handkerchiefs to the ends. For half an hour, they lay suspended between hope and fear. Then the ship disappeared from the sea. There passed two hours among the most cruel reflections, when the master gunner looked up and saw the *Argus* half a league distant, carrying a full press of sail and bearing down upon them. The fifteen survivors were taken up onboard. The commander and the officers onboard rekindled in them the flame of life. Two who later recorded their account of the ordeal concluded that the manner in which they were saved was truly miraculous, and that the finger of Heaven was conspicuous in the event.

As it happened, while I was trying to think about best-case and worst-case scenarios, I read Julian Barnes's essay about Géricault's great painting, known to us as *The Raft of the Medusa* (he himself called it *Shipwreck at Sea*). In my heavily truncated paraphrase of the description of what occurred on this raft, you will easily get a sense of the horrors which the people on the raft had to endure. Perhaps you, as with me, found there was an almost irresistible pull of allegory here: Yeah, we are all on the raft.

There is, however, an outstanding question to be resolved, which is: Would this be an allegory for the best-case scenario, or would it be an allegory for the worst-case scenario? The worst case might not be so bad: It tends to show that things will get worse before they get better, but they will get better. The best case? Well, that might not be so good. If the best that can possibly happen is that the *Argus*, the frigate on the horizon, will show up, then less good than that, the frigate may *not* show up.

I think that the fact that one can ask which case the allegory might apply to is quite telling. It's telling us we are not trapped in our narrative, the way that the poor souls on the raft were trapped in theirs. The causes of that disaster were both ultimate and proximate. There was bad navigation to begin with, and the frigate struck the reef; there was also bad organization in the immediate, consequent actions of the men onboard. But above all, the proximate causes were our behavior towards each other. This is the crux of the allegory, and what it ought to mean to us.

One tenth of the people on that raft survived. The *Medusa* set sail in July 1816, and all this happened soon after that. What was operating on that raft was our famous, indefatigable, relentless desire to preserve ourselves. With cooperation, it's easily possible that nine tenths of that hundred and fifty rather than one tenth would have survived. I think that what I would like to take from this rather double-focused look at the best and worst that might be to come—I would like to take the story of *The Raft of the Medusa* as a morality tale, a cautionary tale. I think what it's telling us is that if we don't cooperate, we're screwed. We're sunk. We have to live our lives on the raft as a contest of generosity, and that way, and only that way, we might survive.

ONRUSH

Serge Brussolo
Translated by Edward Gauvin

He went home, clothes stiff from the underground winter. He could still feel the sting of ice shards on his cheeks, and his chapped lips were bleeding. He made himself some coffee, very sweet, and tried to warm his hands by caressing the mug's porcelain sides. He had his first hallucination as he walked diagonally across the kitchen. The tiled floor crumbled beneath his feet, revealing a liquid expanse. The tiles broke loose, one from the next, sinking into the dark pool that seemed to spread beneath the floor of the apartment. David leapt to one side, blinked his eyes. The image vanished, and the kitchen floor revealed itself to be untouched. There was no hole, no secret lake… He sat down, legs trembling, and passed a hand over his face. The hallucination had been so realistic he'd felt that he was balancing over a chasm, the tenant of a hut on stilts that was falling to pieces. He wanted another sip, but was appalled to find it tasted like seawater. Seaweed floated on the surface. In the depths of the mug, sugar had been replaced with silt. He knew that if he kept staring at the mug, he'd soon see fish swimming around the spoon. He closed his eyes, covered his face with his hand. The smell of salt and mud blossomed from the coffeepot's spout, filling the room. He forced himself to breathe slowly. He knew these symptoms; they were an alarm signal his unconscious sent out to announce a deep dive. Normally, he would've jumped on the phone and called Marianne. She'd have come over right away with her little suitcase, her bottles of glucose, her IV drips. She would've assisted him while he lost consciousness, seeing to the continued function of his deserted body. He began to rise, but changed his mind. No, he shouldn't. If he told her he was about to go under, she'd rush to bring him an injection…

He took a deep breath to banish the ball of worry forming at the tip of his sternum. What he was about to do infringed upon the fundamental safety rules of diving, but he couldn't help it, he wanted to see Nadia again. Gently, he opened his eyes. The hallucination had worn off. The mug held only cold coffee now. The tiled floor was intact and afforded no glimpse of secret seas. *It's too soon,* a voice murmured to him. *You're still too weak to try another descent, you haven't recovered yet.* He got to his feet. The apartment was pitching a bit, like a ship on a rising sea. The objects on the sideboards, the mantels, came and went, obeying the movements of the swell. The building was taking to the ocean, slicing through the tide with its redbrick prow. David could hear the regular slap of waves against the walls of the ground floor. He knew that if he opened the curtains, he would see foam streaming down the windowpanes. The dive was always heralded by maritime hallucinations. He almost lost his balance going down the hallway. Chairs fell over, dishes slid about in the cupboards, books tumbled from the shelves. He'd left the port; now the apartment building was braving the first breakers of the high seas. Used to it as he was, David still felt nausea. He staggered toward the bathroom. The faucets of the sink and tub had turned themselves on, pouring out green, frothy water that smelled of iodine. Gray fish flopped about in the toilet, slapping the porcelain with their powerful fins. David felt his head spin, felt fear knot his stomach. The illusion was too strong. The convincing, almost palpable images presaged a dive of great depth. If he gave into the trance, he could easily sleep for two weeks, maybe more. In a few days, he would become dehydrated, then slide into a coma. More than one diver had died that way. Diving alone was throwing yourself down a well with a stone tied around your neck. He had to call Marianne.

Seized with vertigo, he dragged himself toward the bedroom and collapsed across the bed like a shipwreck victim. The apartment seemed to be hitting twenty-foot troughs, and huge waves came crashing down on the tiled floor with the thunder of a waterfall. The smell of iodine was everywhere now. The salt-starched bedsheets stuck to David's fingers. He tried to remember where he'd hidden the bottles of glucose. Oh, he could jimmy up a homemade rig that would keep him alive for a while, but none of these pitiful precautions would help against the dangers of a deep-sea dive. This time, the call of the deep was terrifying. David felt the apartment warping from the assault of the invisible maelstrom. Soon the floorboards would give way, and he would sink into the blue waters. He would go deeper than ever before; he could feel it. His feet weighed tons, they would tug him downward like the lead ballast of the first undersea explorers. His body was becoming heavy, immovable. His limbs would recover their give only once he was submerged. He had to dive, let himself be sucked in…

He undressed, tearing off his clothes like remnants of an old skin after molting. With one trembling hand, he tore open the sterile pouch with the IV needle and its transparent little tube. Had he set the timer? His vision blurred and the digits on the counter danced a saraband around the buttons. He quickly arranged the lines, plugged the device in, and stuck the needle in the hollow of his arm. It hurt. He tore off some surgical tape with his teeth, slapped it flat over the insertion point, and lay down on his back. He was nauseated. His visual acuity decreased, as if night were flooding the apartment. He knew he was already going down. This would be his greatest dive, he could feel it: a journey to the heart of the abyss, into the black hole of the great deep, where he had never before set foot. Where maybe no one had ever set foot. He would let the weight of his rancor drag him down, all the sadness of murdered dreams. He was going straight to the bottom, cleaving the ocean depths like a diver caparisoned in brass and lead, his gleaming helmet tracing through the liquid night a wake of humming bubbles. *I'm coming!* he thought, closing his eyes. The pillow lapped at his neck, the froth of the sheet licked his loins. He sank and nothing could keep him at the surface anymore.

Suddenly, everything was blue.

MARS(EILLAISE)

Purdey Lord Kreiden

First I was intoxicated with rubbing my pussy
  Lightly against the chair upon which I was sitting,
    Rocking back and forth for ages then with running
      Around my grandparents' pillars to get dizzy
        Then with sitting on my legs for a long time
      To get my limbs all numb with les fourmis after
    That I got hooked on baby bottle filled with coca
  Cola then milk then on drinking anything out of a baby
  Bottle and on getting fed by my grandmother without
  Having to hold the fork myself to my mouth
  Then I discovered masturbation that occupied me
  For a while then I was hooked on the feeling that
      Ran through me when I rubbed my leg against
        Maxime Givetogod's legs in grammar school
          Then I got hooked on what the other kids could think
        Of me the whole time the masturbation thing
    Was a big thing and never sobering, I remember
      Doing it when my mom came to sit on my bed
      Before bedtime, at lunchtime after school and
        Before going back, through jeans that I wore out
          Until there was a washed out pearl-colored angel
            Ring at the crotch of all my jeans then it was herbal
            Cigarettes oh I forgot in between that I was hooked
          On reading my writings to the class, they were
          Fairytales which I generously sprinkled with the names
    Of the kids I wanted to be liked by, and I would write
    One each day at lunch break, and one each night

So I could read it the next morning to the class,
That was a big thrill after the herbal cigarettes
I was drunk on letting a small piece of my underwear
Appear so that the boys in my school would look
At my butt and try to touch it as I passed
At the same time it drunkened me to sit on those boys'
Knees and when they patted my ass with clumzy paws
And to tongue the air at them in arts and crafts classes;
Then I didn't sober and I went straight to smoking Chesterfield
Reds and then I was drunk on drinks, I drank vodka for the first
Time and went to music classes drunk after lunch and my conception
Of the universe changed into a calm bowl of pale porridge;
Suddenly life was a melody I could panflute anywhere if
Only I had a vodka-caramel bottle in my bag, which I always
Did, hidden in a plastic water bottle then I was on more and more
Vodka, I drank it in the bus to Marseille in the morning then I did an
Ethylic coma after that I got drunk on ecstasy pills the first one
I ever had my god the sun rose after ten or twelve hours
Of dancing and I've never felt so happy in my entire life
And Modeselektor was playing sounds in between ecstasy pills
I thought about them so hard I finally got hooked on an energy drink
Called Dark Dog, which is now forbidden, and which tasted
Like a very friendly sour cherry. At the same time I was drunk by
White nights and taking pictures in the early mornings
When the streets were asleep and then I was on Paradise
Which is a mix of mdma and mescaline and when Louie
Gave it to me for the first time he laced it with grenadine
And we walked on the port to go to the movies and the sea
And the people and the sun all looked like they were
In 3D, and I was on being in love with my gay best friend,
Which was a big thrill then I was hooked on so much coffee
My heart almost exploded then I drank wine and beer and I got drugged
By merely dancing until clubs closed in the morning
And my eyes remained closed too as I walked out of them
In Paris (by that time I had started to be addicted to living alone
For the first time and eating only pasta with nothing on it
And drinking and drinking and my days were bright) Soon

I got also hooked on eating raw meat and steak tartares
And going to the restaurant each night then I was addicted
To dancing and being seen as I did and pretending
To ignore I was and at the same time I was hooked
On a german composer guy called Dominik and I would drink half
A bottle of tequila in the lobby of his building before gravitating
To the seventh floor which sheltered his house and the whole time
I was intoxicated by fucking all the time and then I was
On mdma and then I was on Biche and we were hooked
On speed and mdma and beer and amazement and whiskey
And trains and cities we barely looked at every night
We would drink a bottle a whole bottle of whiskey and erase our
Memories then I was making collages and then I was high
On being very sick and almost dying that took three
Weeks to happen at the exact same time of the year three
Years ago and I died for Easter day and resurrected just
Like him for a week at the hospital I was high on morphine
And the nurses all laughed at me because they thought I was addicted
To ketamine, then I was home high on sodomy because I'd been advised
By the medicinal corps not to have any sort of sexual intercourse
And I was then on whiskey and on Biche again and then
I was given Lamaline suppositories for the pain
In my belly so I started being addicted to that and then
Once I couldn't get them without prescription so the pharmacist
Gave me three boxes of codeinated paracetamol pills
Instead and I took them with disbelief and I've been amorously
Taking them twice a day ever since; that was three years ago
And now I still can't write sober and it sucks I think but I don't
Know if it does because writing all this to you amazes me and I
Think it's a miracle a miracle my fantasy is we are silent

BOMBS

Ezekiel Caligiuri

Day One

They locked us down the same day somebody planted the bombs that went off at the Boston Marathon. We all knew it was coming. We usually did. We got our two lockdowns a year no matter what. Routine lockups were anticipated for months sometimes, with the gossipmongers anticipating them at every count. I used to love them. They were breaks for guys from their prison jobs as welders or machinists with faces and clothes full of soot, or janitors wiping snot and shit from walls. They were breaks from all the tension of maintaining aloofness and indifference, hoping for some rest.

It takes a certain spiritual strength to get by through long stretches in the joint; that, or an ignorance that at times can seem like the same thing. I often used my days locked in my cell as a time of spiritual restoration. It gave us a break from having to talk to each other about all the same stuff we talked about every day. I used to need a break from my time, and the trade-off was the modest stress of getting my cell turned upside down. But lately it seemed like we were going on and coming off of lockdowns every few weeks.

This time we just hoped we'd get our canteen before they dropped the notice of the shakedown. The house was so dry, people were paying four times the cost of ramen noodles and beef summer sausages. I didn't have food in my canteen bag except for a single pack of noodles, a third of a roll of crackers, and a sealed pack of chicken. We were just a day from getting our commissary when they slipped the memo on our bars. It was the usual presumptuous memo: *Thank you for your cooperation.* The news ignited the usual groans and guttural sounds in response to another in our never-ending string of disappointments. One guy screamed until his voice went hoarse, "You are an evil person, Sgt. _____!" Then

---

Ezekiel Caligiuri won the 2015 PEN Prison Writing Award for Memoir.

there were those who used it to congratulate themselves: "I told you. Didn't I tell you they were going to do this?" I was surrounded by guys who didn't speak during lockdowns. The first night, my friend CF on my right said, "They're bogus for this." I didn't hear his voice much after that.

On my left was the old man China, who is really only a couple of years older than I am, and not Chinese but Laotian. He ran around south Minneapolis at the same time I did. He was twenty years of the way through his life sentence, and wore an extra-scratchy personality on the outside, probably just to protect his sanity. On the other side of CF was J, who was fourteen when he got his life sentence, twenty-six when they gave it to him again. Next to J there was Preach, who was seventeen when he got his life sentence. Next to China was F, he was seventeen; next to him another, seventeen as well. Below us was the twenty-year-old kid who was one of the first to get life without the possibility of parole; next to him, Johnny, twenty years into his life stint. These guys considered me, with only ten years left, halfway out the door.

The sting of time had left marks on all of us, but the others still liked lockdowns, called them vacations. It was easier when I was younger and didn't think I deserved very much. I was twenty-two once, and these bricks didn't know me yet. This time, I kind of panicked. The timing was just bad and I wasn't prepared. I had hardly any food in my bag, and what they fed us was the lowest and most vile form of food, frozen and stashed somewhere for weeks or months. All my water bottles were empty, so I was consigned to the noxious chemical taste of unfiltered tap water flowing from the old well through the hundred-year-old pipes. I had a bag of dirty laundry and hardly enough underwear to get me through the next few days. I was frustrated because I would lose typing days just weeks from a deadline. And I would miss poetry class on Wednesday night, one of the only nights in my week where I felt a release from the strictures that held me in place.

I figured, though, if they shook us down right away in the morning, I could spend those days writing and maybe finish my book. I was reading *A Right to Be Hostile*, about the public school-to-prison pipeline. It was taking me unusually long to read, because I would get angry after every few pages and put it down. I might have the time now. It might keep me from obsessing over the food and the water and the treatment. I was better than this place, and I had proved it to myself over and over. I had told my family this so often, they were tired of hearing about it.

I had been through so many lockdowns during my prison bid, or bit, or stretch, or piece, or whatever we call it. We used to cook meals in our hot pots and hand booze back and forth in the middle of the night. I had been through the fourteen-day lockdown after the old bruiser stomped that kid into a puddle. I had withstood a couple during the hottest weeks of summer. I'd had them where some wicked woman crouched down and counted our socks and dirty drawers and read letters from home, and when they brought dogs through, leaving paw prints on my blankets. I'd been in them during holidays and during prison softball championships. I was locked down on my thirty-second birthday, and had a card signed by all of my friends sent down the tier one cell at a time. I'd had visitors turned away without explanation. Guys even used to talk about the monthlong routines going back to the nineties. The guys in B West broke dozens of windows with cartons of milk during their lockdown in '04. In 1983 they broke nine hundred of them. Lockdowns could be tough, but we created stories from them: They were part of the communal endurance that made us know we could still be human. But hopefully this one would be over in a few days.

I have made a bid of staying reserved and cautious about the explosive elements of myself—a bomb of unexpressed knowledge and feeling about all I have seen, about the way people are treated. I just didn't know how long before it would explode from me. I wanted to vent and yell something ignorant out of my bars, but that would just make me sound like so many other guys, shouting like they were children reacting to punishment from their parents. I couldn't waste the spiritual energy, I needed it all. It made me feel soft, though, or scared, because I couldn't react the way my heart told me I should.

I sat and watched TV. The same footage of the bombing played in a loop. It reminded me a little of 9/11; I was in a cell for that, too. We waited in limbo as all the networks brought their experts aboard to shill their version of fear. We were supposed to be scared all over again. We were supposed to pull out our lists of usual suspects and choose one or two to be angry at; my list was different from theirs. I tried to stay detached from the footage, as though that was a world of fiction and these things didn't really happen, people didn't blow other people up. But I couldn't help but feel the drop, the tapping of footsteps on the other side of the future, the rattling shifting of how we see our world. These shifts happen so often now.

I watched anyway. I stayed up late, flipped between the NBA and continuous shots of the bombings. There were scenarios everywhere: reports of a third bombing at the JFK Library that was later declared unrelated, possibilities of copycat bombings, and a fertilizer plant in West

Texas that blew up in the night. During commercials I dug through my footlockers to make sure everything was hidden where I needed it to be, to make sure I had an accounting of all my extra T-shirts and drawers, and all the extra hygiene products I used for currency. I had way too many books. I was used to being told this; most of the space was taken up by my notebooks, a collection that was still growing.

Day Two

The guard woke me up by stuffing a brown paper bag with cereal and two smashed boiled eggs between my bars. I had one of the feverish and debilitating headaches that had plagued me since I was a child and that I still got regularly. I took the two milks and flung them over the tier like bombs with no intended targets, just to get the possibility of rotten milk stench as far from my cell as possible. I heard them smack against the floor, but I couldn't see where they landed. I had to drink my coffee with tepid water I got from the hot water button on my sink because I had melted my hot pot a few weeks before. I tried to sleep, but I felt an urgency to get back up to re-hide the things I'd already hidden. My first thoughts were about *something* I had hidden that I knew could cost me the most. Without getting it out of my mind, I would never be able to concentrate enough to read, let alone write. I went back and forth between throwing it off the tier and manning up and dealing with it. I used the reflection in my toenail clipper to look back and forth on the galley for the police, hoping they would hurry up and shake us down.

I'm used to a cell. It has become natural to me. There are secrets it keeps without emotion attached to them. I never expected fifteen years would feel like this—the constant flux of open and closed, the clicking and crash of locking myself into a box over and over, inhale, exhale, until I'm complicit and even comfortable with it. It is my space. The cell, the cage, my kennel, my box—six by eight by nine to the very back, with crisscrossing steel bars, like at Alcatraz or San Quentin, that cast checkered shadows in the rooms, connected by a break a human being opens at certain times of the day by pulling an old steel lever. I essentially live in a bathroom stall. My head rests a foot and a half from my sink, two and a half feet from a stainless steel toilet (the doctor here told me once I had to piss all the time because I had to look at that toilet all day, every day).

It is during these breaks that the cell and I get to know each other, become a part of the same history, connected to a whole block of cells anchored in a rectangular row of concrete that runs from hallway to showers in perfect rows four tiers high. I like it dark when I am by myself, so I hung a sheet from wall to wall to completely block out my cell bars. When guards came by, they asked me: "What are you doing back there?" I was just reading or watching TV. I tried to meditate, but it always came back to hunger, then to hostility. In some ways the cell is the perfect enclosure for the single human being, alone with God. I often think I might die in one of these.

CNN was still showing the bomb sequences. Day two brought all of the human interest stories, the deaths, the paralysis. The experts were still pinning it on the likelihood that Al Qaeda or some other international group was lurking insidiously behind it all. While I drank my instant coffee, they were trying to draw connections between the bombings and the latest failed gun control bill in the House. ESPN streamed live tweets of reactions from professional athletes. Catchphrases started coming out like they always do—"Boston Strong"—and hashtags: "#Bombings," "#GoSox!"

I still had the headache when they brought lunch. It wouldn't go away—they never did, until they shook me down and the doors opened and my blood pressure dropped. Just hearing and smelling the food carts roll in made me a sick kind of anxious. A very tall African guard with a goofy smile on his face, who is always trying to carry on the silliest dialogues with inmates, tried to hand me a cardboard tray with some kind of rectangular patty, four tater tots, and about fifteen gray peas. I ate the bread and politely told him to keep the tray. My guy down the tier got mad at me for not giving it to him.

Most moments during a bid are forgotten. It would be impossible to keep together all the scattered moments of hurt or disappointment, of boredom or indifference. Until they get so congested together that they become the *sickness*. I was already sick. I had been for so long. This kind of sickness kills in slow motion. Rot. I spent most of the afternoon eating ibuprofen and listening to my stomach grumble. I read two pages of *A Right to Be Hostile*, but it was still hard to concentrate. I ate the food I had and felt temporarily satiated.

CNN cut in with news that an envelope with ricin, sent to some congressman, was intercepted. Then they broke in that another envelope had been snatched on its way to the president. I wanted to write, but my head hurt and I couldn't concentrate on anything other than the experts on TV spending hours explaining how the poison was made. I got a letter from my aunt, something abstract and separate from this place. Dinner came around again, meatballs. "Hey Preach, take this garbage." I ate some more bread. By late afternoon they had somebody in custody for the ricin envelopes. It came with the news that Congress had struck down the new gun control bill. Lines attached to laundry bags with toilet paper and noodles in them zipped by my cell to someone down the tier.

That night, the Ken Burns documentary about the Central Park Five came on PBS. It was the last thing I needed to see, another dark example of how the justice system fucks and manipulates people, especially poor young people. I watched an unrelenting public execute those boys through the media. Maybe it came from everything that was happening, but I cried for all of the years those boys got stolen from them. Maybe I was really crying about the years I'd lost. I was exhausted all over again. I was tired of being a slave.

The nurse came by with my headache medication. When did I start taking medication, anyway? I used to be so much stronger. Another documentary came on afterward, *The War Next Door,* about the lost War on Drugs. I gritted my teeth and let myself get dizzy. My hands got numb from clenching. I was tired of being sick.

I guess I was angry. I felt small under the forces I felt so oppressed by: the police, prosecutors, judges, the Department of Corrections, right on down to the people that made our food, the guards that dropped it off to us, and a general public that has accepted all of this as just, never understanding it could happen to them and their families as well. In the beginning, when I was still young to this, I read books written by men in prison who got out and went back to lives as artists and activists, or started organizations. I saw myself as someone like that, stronger and incapable of being hurt by these years, fortified by the experience instead. I believed in a narrative of transformation and metamorphosis.

Lately, I'd started to see things differently. Lately, and especially on that night, I felt like maybe transforming and reemerging were really just meant for an earlier set of prisoners, before mass sentencing, and before the prison system became such a powerful industrial force. I thought maybe they should have just given us our OID numbers in the eighth grade so we wouldn't waste any more time dreaming.

I *really* needed them to shake us down in the morning so the pressure in my shoulders and the thump in my head might go away.

Day Three

But they didn't shake us down. I was awakened by the nurse bringing me my pills. My headache woke up with me. I got up again, checking my spots, contemplating moving that *something* around again. I decided not to—what will be, will be. The coffee still tasted like fertilizer, a knot throbbed over my right eye, my mouth was dry, and I was starving. I had decided I was done accepting this treatment. I would commit my life to the abolishment of prisons. The food carts came again: Salisbury steak patty, are you fucking serious? The ricin envelope bomber had been released and they were looking for his ex-wife now. They were already setting up vigils for the marathon victims.

I needed to write to fill those nervous days. When I'm working, I'm human. When I'm not, I'm just a monkey that jumps up when a bell rings. Lockdowns used to be a time when I could work, when I could catch up on what I was reading or do homework. But I was sick; I was a monkey from eating next to nothing, and from carrying around the illness that grows up inside of us over all these years. Was this what fifteen years felt like? I took the tray and flung it through my bars out onto the tier, but most of it just hit the bars and left a mess on the floor and the inside of the room. I was too tired to clean it up. "Hey, Preach, you ain't getting this one." I lay down with a towel soaked in cold water wrapped around my head. I dreamt of sickness.

I woke up midafternoon in sweats, extra-sensitive to the smell of trash and shit. Hefty bags tied to the outside of our cells were full of milk cartons and festering trays. It is crazy how so many men get to shitting at the same time, toilets flushing in rhythm. I knew I smelled, too. With detergent and a scrub brush, I washed socks and drawers in my sink. I couldn't help but look at myself in the mirror bolted to the wall. I splashed water over a face that got no cleaner.

When chow came again, I could feel my stomach sucking in. I knew I could eat it, but I also knew as soon as I bit into it, I would be sicker, angrier. Maybe I wasn't really angry, maybe it was just fear that all that transcendence shit I was spouting was fake. Maybe all of these extra years were really just a trick to make me docile and weak. Maybe it didn't matter what a person did in his cell, maybe the force of everything you do loses its power after so long. Maybe I really had lost my spirit, my humanity. I was a caged animal, meant to eat like a beast.

I wanted to ask myself if I had a right to be so hostile. This is prison, it has been since I've known it, since it ever was. So why did it hurt so much now? The lockdown, the food? Was it because I was getting older? Or because I was afraid I had wasted it? Maybe I didn't have time to write the book I'd been trying to finish, or I would never have children. Or because I had finally grown up, but it all came in here—living from lockdown to lockdown, scared they would take the last thing I really needed. Maybe it was because the clock never stops ticking, the future still comes in whatever form it chooses. Or was it because I was tired? Tired of being that passive slave in jailhouse oranges sleepwalking through years.

When I get to feeling like this, there is always an inmate or a teacher or a guard that feels he needs to tell me how much worse it is for prisoners in other places around the world. I tell them: "I know. Those are my people." We are all inextricably linked to each other through these cells, or maybe more so through time. The cell keeps us still; the time takes us to all the different places that change us, hopefully in ways beautiful, but most often in all the ugly ways. Prison has always been this way, I guess. I asked CF once: What if we had been born somewhere else—how do you think our lives would be different? "We'd probably just be in a cell somewhere else," he said, as though this were our natural state. "Some people are meant to be free. Most people aren't." That didn't make me any less tired, or scared, or crazy.

I turned the TV on again and there was surveillance footage of the two alleged marathon bombers. They didn't look like terrorists. In the footage, they wore cargo pants and had bangs spilling out from under baseball caps, and backpacks slung over their shoulders. They looked like high school or college students. They still walked like kids. We saw their blurry faces over and over—the same few shots. Whoever they were, they had to be somewhere watching, knowing it was almost over. It was their one chess move in life, and they had blown up kids and parents, blown the legs off marathon runners. Of all the monsters and monstrous forces in the world, this was how they had chosen to expel their anger? These were the people we were supposed to fear? I wasn't afraid of them. I was more afraid of going crazy in a cell after so many years. I just got the familiar nervous feeling I get whenever I see young people on the verge of inheriting a million years in a place like this. I felt a sorrow, not for these foolish youngsters who left irreparable damage behind them, but for all of the foolish youngsters I've known. Soon we'll be linked to them, too, whether we want to be or not.

While I watched the National Guard with tanks and an ocean of police assembled on every Boston street corner, guys were on the tier heatedly debating the existence of mermaids, watching something on a channel I didn't even know we had. Another section of kids was rapping a Rick Ross song almost deliriously in unison. There was a guy on a tier below me practicing his guitar, strumming the same chord over and over again. As much as I tried to separate myself from them, I couldn't: They were my people.

That night I watched the Central Park jogger documentary again, just for something to rage about. Yeah, I was tired of being a slave. But I was also tired of fighting. Nobody listened. By that evening, they had two brothers identified as the marathon bombers. There was already a slew of family and friends in front of cameras for their own few minutes of fame. It was the way it has always been. Ask the Central Park kids about it.

Day Four

When I woke up again, cops were at my door, there to finally dig through my life. If what I had wasn't hidden well enough—well, then it was too late, I was fucked. The TV was on fire with the news that the older brother had died overnight. He'd been hit by the car the younger brother was driving to flee a gas station robbery. They shut down an entire city for these kids?

They strip-searched me and then brought me down the tier and handcuffed me to a railing next to CF and China and a couple of other guys I had done years and years alongside. All of us with IDs clipped to our T-shirts with our OID numbers as testaments to how long we'd been in our cocoons. One of us considered that between the five of us gathered there, "we've probably been through two hundred lockdowns just between us." Yet there were rookies shaking our rooms down who had never participated in lockdowns before. It was crazy how after so many, I was still nervous. I was supposed to be tougher than this. *Why am I being so soft?* I probably could have asked China what *twenty* years felt like—or what he anticipated the next twenty might be like. He told me he needed a few more days of this.

One by one, guys were uncuffed and brought back to their cells, but I was still there as other prisoners came and were handcuffed next to me. There really wasn't time to be scared now. Several more prisoners were sent back to their cells before a skinny guard with a ridiculous blond mustache pulled up on me. They must have found *it*. I knew I had messed up, I knew I had overthought it. Instead, the guy had the nerve to tell me I had too many notebooks. I just shook my head and slammed the cell door behind me. I saw two seat marks side by side on my mattress. The TV channel had been changed to wrestling. The *something* was secure and safe where I had put it, at least until the next time.

With my headache still lingering, I watched an army hunt down the baby-faced little brother. They started to let the tiers out to take showers. The lockdown was almost over. I could wash the filth from my body, and try to speak in sentences for the first time in a while. By the time I got back, they had the young bomber hiding in a boat in someone's backyard, full of bullet holes. They said he tried to blow himself up, but couldn't. I wanted them to just let the kid die, so they could give us all some finality. By this point I wanted it all to be over. I needed my bid to be over, too.

But of course they didn't let the kid die: They pulled him in, saved him. There would be a trial now. I didn't want to have to choose between two sides, like watching two basketball teams I hate. There would be more news coverage and all sorts of opportunities for others to jump forward and be heroes, but they wouldn't bring anybody back to life or undo any of what was broken. There would be more bombs hidden somewhere or falling from the sky.

It was over—but it wasn't, really. There was still that deadline for the story I was supposed to write, and the deadline couldn't be pushed back. Our OIDs don't come with deadlines, though; they stay with us whether we get out, go crazy, or die. It doesn't matter *when* they give us our number, because we keep it the rest of our lives.

I would spend another night in my cell and it would tell me a secret. It would tell me: There *would* be a transformation. We *would* get transformed into something else, and these moments would be written and remembered as an everlasting part of the metamorphosis. There would be no forgetting them. But tomorrow they would open these breaks, the cell door would open, I would exhale, I would talk to people again, but I would still be angry, and I would still be sick, and I would still be hungry.

THE STAR
by Jarod Roselló

A STAR DESCENDED INTO OUR
LIVING ROOM ONE EVENING

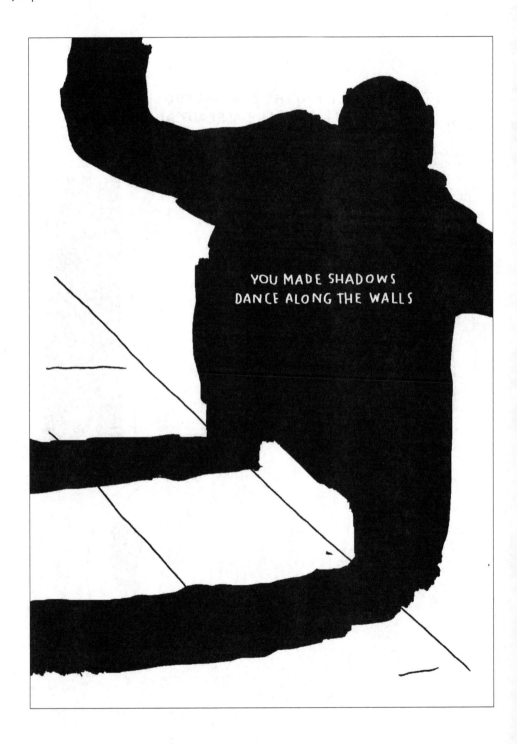

WHERE IT SPUN IN A WOBBLY ELLIPSE
ORBITING SOMETHING UNSEEN

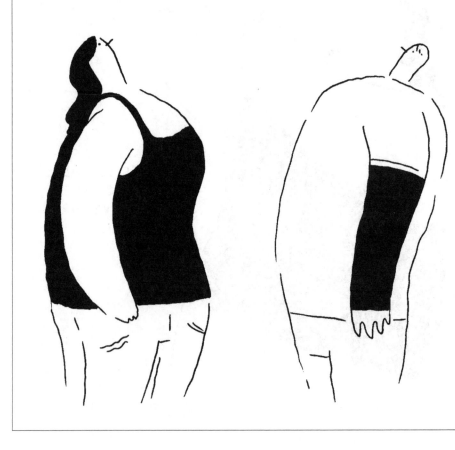

THAT NIGHT, YOU SET A BLANKET ON THE TILE FLOOR
BENEATH THE STAR AND WE LAY DOWN TOGETHER

PARTS OF OUR BODIES TOUCHED

CIRCLING OVERHEAD

EMITTING A FIELD OF LIGHT AND WARMTH

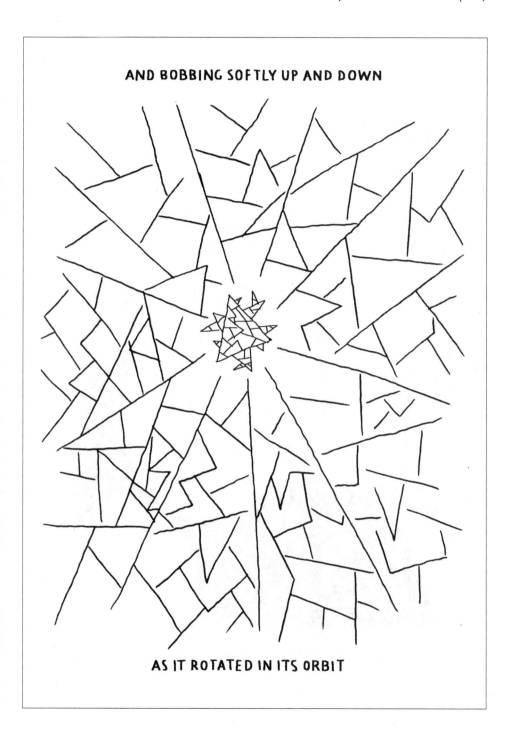

UNANCHORED, BUT TETHERED IN SOME INVISIBLE WAY

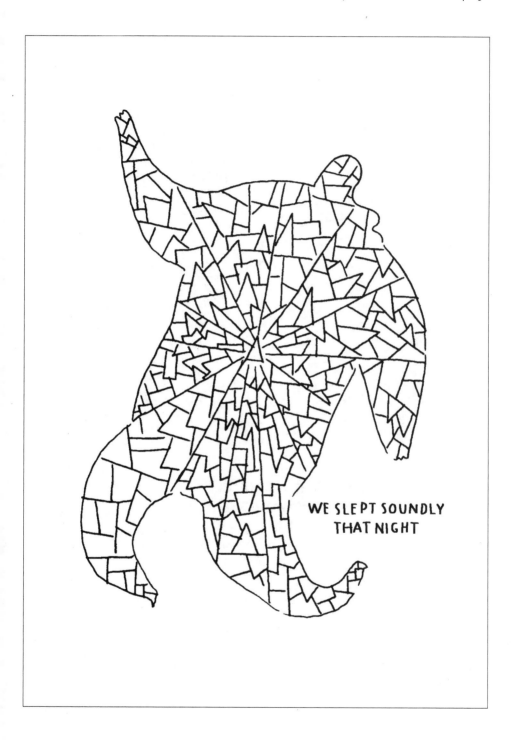

WE SLEPT SOUNDLY
THAT NIGHT

THE PILOT

Russell Edson

Up in a dirty window in a dark room is a star which an old man can see. He looks at it. He can see it. It is the star of the room; an electrical freckle that has fallen out of his head and gotten stuck in the dirt on the window.

He thinks he can steer by that star. He thinks he can use the back of a chair as a ship's wheel to pilot his room through the night.

He says to himself, brave Captain, are you afraid?

Yes, I am afraid; I am not so brave.

Be brave, my Captain.

And all night the old man steers his room through the dark . . .

MAKEDONIJA

Miroslav Penkov

I was born a year after my brother. When I was twelve Mother bore another boy, but it died a baby. Two years after that she had twin girls. We lived in my grandfather's house and worked his land. Our grandpa was a lazy man, the laziest I've known, but he had his reasons. He sat out on the threshold from dusk till after dawn and smoked hashish. He'd let me sit beside him and told me stories of the Turkish times. All through his youth he'd served a Turkish bey, and that bey had broken his back with work enough for seven lifetimes. So now, in freedom, Grandpa refused to do as much as wipe his ass. That's what he'd say. "I have your father to wipe my ass," he'd say, and hit the smoke. He drew maps of Bulgaria in the dust, enormous as it had been more than five centuries ago, before the Turks had taken over our land. He'd draw a circle around the north and say, "This is called Moesia. This is where we live, free at last, thanks to the Russian brothers." Then he'd circle the south. "This is Thrace. It stayed part of the Turkish Empire for seven years after the north was freed, but now we are one, united. And this," he'd say and circle farther south, "is Macedonia. Home to Bulgarians, but still under the fez." He'd brush fingers along the lines and watch the circles for a long time, put arrows where he thought the Russians should invade and crosses where battles should be waged. Then he'd spit in the dust and draw the rest of Europe and circle it, and circle Africa and Asia. "One day, siné, all these continents will be Bulgarian again. And maybe the seas." Again he'd hit the smoke and sometimes he'd let me take a drag, too, because a little herb, he'd say, never hurt a child.

And now, in bed, I suddenly long to fill up my lungs with all that burning so that my head gets light and empty. Instead, I fill up with memories of things long gone the way a gourd fills up with water from rain.

Our father was a bitter man, having to kiss his in-law's hand before each meal. Father beat us plenty with his chestnut stick and I remember him happy on a single day in 1905, when we celebrated twenty years since the north had been united with the south. He sat me down with my brother, poured each a mortar of red wine, and made us drink to the bottom, like men. He told us that when next we got our Macedonia back, he'd fill the mortars up with rakia.

Father was lost in the Balkan war, seven years after. I'd like to think he fell near Edirne, a heroic death, but I won't blame him if he just chose not to return. I hope he rests in peace. When Grandpa died, it fell to me and Brother to care for the women. We worked the fields of others, cut hay, herded the village sheep. And everyone spoke of a new war, bigger than the Balkan, and that war, too, at last, reached our village. Men with guns set up camp on the square, recruiting soldiers. They said all boys of such and such age had to enlist. They said if we helped Germany win, the Germans would let us take back the land that Serbs, and Greeks, and Romanians had stolen from us after the Balkan wars. The Germans would even let us take Macedonia back from the Turks and be complete once and for all. Our mother wept and kissed my hands and then my brother's. She said, "I can't lose both my sons in this war. But I can't let you hide and shame our blood." She sent the twins to milk two sheep, then put a copper of milk before me and one before my brother. Whoever drank his copper first would get to stay home and run the house. The other would go to war. I drank as though I'd never drink again. I chugged. I quaffed. I inhaled that milk. When I was done, I saw my brother had barely touched lips to his.

Dear God. Why now? Have I no other worries? I lie and I remember and listen to the falling snow from this old and foolish letter. I feel the cold of the mountain and see my brother holding that copper still full of liquid snow. For heaven's sake, Brother. Drink.

from *DEEPSTEP COME SHINING*

C. D. Wright

In the hither world I lead you willingly along the light-bearing

paths. In the hither world I offer a once-and-for-all thing,

opaque and revelatory, ceaselessly burning. Anyone who has

ever been through a fire knows how devastating it can be.

The furniture lost, books collected over thirty years, the

mother's white piano. I was there. I know.

CONTRIBUTORS

Amber Atiya recently released a chapbook, *the fierce bums of doo-wop*. Her honors include a Poets House fellowship and inclusion in 2015's *Best New Poets*. Atiya's writing has been featured in *Black Renaissance Noire, Bone Bouquet, Boston Review,* and *Nepantla: A Journal Dedicated to Queer Poets of Color.*

Kehinde Bademosi's forthcoming memoir, *The Exodus,* explores his background as a Pentacostal preacher in Nigeria. In 2008, Bademosi created Orange Academy, Africa's first practical school of brand experience. His social media platform "Is Anyone in Africa" connects people dealing with sexuality and HIV issues.

Eric Banks has served as the senior editor of *Artforum,* editor in chief of *Bookforum,* and president of the National Book Critics Circle. Banks's writing has been featured in *The New York Times Book Review, the Financial Times, Slate,* and *The Wall Street Journal.*

Steven Bley was inspired to start documenting abandoned places after visiting a deserted hotel in 2009. Bley also takes portraits, and has completed photo essays entitled "Sawyer: Year One" and "25 Mirrors." He is based in northern New Jersey.

Serge Brussolo has written almost two hundred books. He experiments with various genres, but he is best known as one of France's premier science fiction writers. In 2009, his popular novel *Les Emmurés* was adapted into the film *Walled In.*

Ezekiel Caligiuri was the winner of the 2015 PEN Prison Writing Contest in memoir for "Bombs." He is an original member of the inmate-created Stillwater Writer's Collective and the B.R.I.D.G.E. Trust Partnership. Caligiuri's memoir, *This Is Where I Am,* is forthcoming from University of Minnesota Press.

Karissa Chen is currently completing a Fulbright fellowship in Taiwan. Her writing has appeared or is forthcoming in numerous publications, including *Gulf Coast, VIDA Web, Guernica, The Toast,* and *PANK.* In 2013, she published her first chapbook, *Of Birds and Lovers.*

Seungja Choi's work focuses on Korea's conflicts during the 1980s. An anthology of her poems, *Portrait of a Suburbanite,* was published in English in 2015 by the University of Hawaii Press. Choi's translated poems include "Already I," "Toward You," and "A Self-Portrait."

Edwidge Danticat came to the United States from Haiti when she was twelve years old. She won a National Book Critics Circle Award for her memoir *Brother, I'm Dying,* and her collection of short stories *Krik? Krak!* was a National Book Award finalist. Her novel *Claire of the Sea Light* was shortlisted for the Andrew Carnegie Excellence in Fiction Award in 2014.

Thomas Drake formerly served as a senior executive of the NSA, and is a decorated United States Air Force and Navy veteran. In 2006, he gave *The Baltimore Sun* information about the NSA's Trailblazer Project. Drake was the 2011 recipient of the Ridenhour Prize for Truth-Telling.

Russell Edson (1935-2014) was a poet, playwright, and novelist. He was honored three times with NEA Creative Writing Fellowships, as well as a Whiting Award and a Guggenheim Fellowship. His collections of poetry include *See Jack, The Rooster's Wife: Poems,* and *The Tormented Mirror.*

Mona Eltahawy is an Egyptian-American freelance journalist, writer, and activist. Her essays and op-eds on Egypt, the Islamic world, and women's rights have appeared in *The Washington Post* and *The New York Times.* Her first book, *Headscarves and Hymens: Why the Middle East Needs a Sexual Revolution,* was published in 2015.

Martín Espada is a poet, editor, essayist, and translator who has published more than fifteen books, most recently *Vivas to Those Who Have Failed*. Espada's many honors include an American Book Award, the National Hispanic Cultural Center Literary Award, the Shelley Memorial Award, and a Guggenheim Fellowship. His book, *The Republic of Poetry*, was a finalist for the Pulitzer Prize. Espada teaches at the University of Massachusetts Amherst.

Laura Esquivel is the author of the novel *Como agua para chocolate* (Like Water for Chocolate), which has been translated into thirty-five languages and was on *The New York Times* bestseller list for a year. Other works by her include *Íntimas suculencias, Estrellita marinera, Malinche*, and her latest novel, *A Lupita le gustaba planchar*. Esquivel has won several prizes as a screenwriter and as a novelist.

Aminatta Forna is the award-winning author of three novels and a memoir, *The Devil That Danced on the Water*. In 2014, Forna won a Donald Windham-Sandy M. Campbell Literature Prize from Yale University. She is currently the Lannan Foundation Chair of Poetics at Georgetown University and a professor of creative writing at Bath Spa University.

Edward Gauvin has received fellowships and residencies from PEN America and PEN England, the NEA, the Fulbright program, the Lannan Foundation, Villa Gillet, the Centre National du Livre, and Ledig House. His translations have appeared in *The New York Times, Subtropics, Tin House, Conjunctions*, and *The Southern Review*.

Kimiko Hahn is the author of nine collections of poetry, most recently *Brain Fever* and *Toxic Flora*. Hahn has received many awards, including an NEA Fellowship, a Shelley Memorial Award, an American Book Award, and the PEN/Voelcker Award for Poetry in 2008. She is currently a professor at Queens College.

Joy Harjo is the author of many books including *Crazy Brave* and *Conflict Resolution for Holy Beings*. Among her accolades are the Wallace Stevens Award in Poetry, a Guggenheim Fellowship, and the 2002 PEN/Open Book Award for *A Map to the Next World: Poetry and Tales*. Harjo is at work on a musical that celebrates indigenous peoples' contributions to American music.

Nicky Harman is an active contributor to the Chinese literature translation website, Paper Republic. Her most recent translations include *Paper Tiger* by Xu Zhiyuan, *Sissy Zhong* by Yan Ge, *January: Bridges* by Dorothy Tse, and *Crystal Wedding* by Xu Xiaobin. Harman won a PEN Translation Fund Grant in 2006 for her translation of *Striking Root* by Han Dong.

Shireen Hassim has written and edited several books, including *No Shortcuts to Power: African Women in Politics and Policymaking* and *Women's Organizations and Democracy in South Africa: Contesting Authority*, which won the Victoria Schuck Award for Best Book on Women and Politics from the American Political Science Association. Her most recent book is *The ANC Women's League*.

Michael Hofmann won the 2014 PEN Translation Prize for his translation of *The Emperor's Tomb* by Joseph Roth. He has been awarded several awards as a poet and translator, including a Cholmondeley Award, an IMPAC Dublin Literary Award, an Oxford-Weidenfeld Translation Prize, and a Helen and Kurt Wolff Translator's Prize. He teaches at the University of Florida.

Cathy Park Hong is the author of *Engine Empire, Translating Mo'um,* and *Dance Dance Revolution,* which was chosen for the Barnard Women Poets Prize. She is the recipient of a Fulbright Fellowship, a National Endowment for the Arts Fellowship and a New York Foundation for the Arts Fellowship. She teaches at Sarah Lawrence College.

Ishion Hutchinson's collection *Far District: Poems* received the 2011 PEN/Joyce Osterweil Award. He is also the author of the chapbook *Bryan's Bay.* Hutchinson's work has appeared in *The Los Angeles Review, Callaloo, The Caribbean Review of Books,* and *Poetry International.* He teaches at Cornell University.

Rashidah Ismaili is the author of the play *Rice Keepers,* which was staged in 2006 at the American Museum. She is also the author of *Autobiography of the Lower East Side, Cantata for Jimmy,* and *Missing in Action and Presumed Dead: Poems,* among others. She lives in New York City.

Cormac James's latest novel, *The Surfacing,* was published in 2015. He is also the author of the novel *Track and Field,* and has published short fiction in *Columbia, Phoenix Irish Short Stories,* and the *Dublin Review.*

Kazuki Kaneshiro made his literary debut in 1998 with *Revolution No. 3,* which won the Shosetsu Gendai Prize for New Writers. In 2000, Kaneshiro won the Naoki Prize for *GO.* The novel's popular film adaptation went on to win major awards in Japan.

Roy Kesey was awarded a 2015 PEN/Heim Translation Fund Grant for his translation of *The Cousins* by Aurora Venturini. He is the author of the short story collection *Any Deadly Thing* and the novel *Pacazo.* His writing and translations have appeared in almost a hundred magazines and anthologies, including *Best American Short Stories* and *New Sudden Fiction.*

Won-Chung Kim's writings include *The Dictionary of Cultural Literacy* and *I Thought It Was A Door.* He has translated ten books of Korean poetry, including Chiha Kim's *Heart's Agony,* and *Cracking the Shell: Three Korean Ecopoets.* He is a professor of English literature, specializing in American poetry, ecological literature, and translation, at Sungkyunkwan University in Seoul, South Korea.

Lee Klein received a 2015 PEN/Heim Translation Fund Grant for his translation of Horacio Castellanos Moya's *Revulsion: Thomas Bernhard in San Salvador.* He is the author of the novel *The Shimmering Go-BeTween.* His writing and translations have appeared in *Harper's, The Best American Nonrequired Reading 2007,* and many other journals and anthologies.

Yusef Komunyakaa is the author of seventeen books of poetry, including *Neon Vernacular,* for which he won the Pulitzer Prize. His other honors include the Ruth Lilly Poetry Prize, the Poetry Society of America's Shelley Memorial Award, and the Wallace Stevens Award. His most recent book is *The Emperor of the Water Clocks.* Komunyakaa teaches at New York University.

Purdey Lord Kreiden is a translator and poet. Her poetry has been featured in the Claudius App, *3AM Magazine, Gobbet,* and the *Yalobusha Review.* She is the author of *Children of the Bad Hour,* and her co-translation of *En ménage* by Joris-Karl Huysmans is forthcoming.

Amitava Kumar's latest book, *Lunch with a Bigot*, is a collection of his literary essays and reportage published in 2015. Kumar's other works include *A Matter of Rats, A Foreigner Carrying in the Crook of His Arm a Tiny Bomb,* and *Evidence of Suspicion.* He is a professor of English at Vassar College.

Lo Kwa Mei-en's debut book of poems, *Yearling,* won the 2013 Kundiman Poetry Prize. *The Bees Make Money in the Lion,* winner of the Cleveland State University Poetry Center Open Competition, was published in spring 2016.

Bob Morris's memoir *Bobby Wonderful* was published in 2015. He has worked as a columnist for the Sunday Styles section of *The New York Times* and as a commentator for NPR's *All Things Considered.* Morris has also received honors from the American Library Association and Lambda Literary.

Horacio Castellanos Moya is a Salvadoran novelist and journalist who has worked for magazines and newspapers in several countries. He has published eleven novels, five short story collections, and a book of essays. He teaches creative writing and media in the department of Spanish and Portuguese at the University of Iowa.

Zanele Muholi is a South African photographer and activist. In 2015, the Brooklyn Museum's exhibit *Isibonelo/Evidence* featured eighty-seven of her works, including the *Faces and Phases* portrait series. She is the winner of the 2016 ICP Infinity Award for documentary and photojournalism.

Takami Nieda received a 2015 PEN/Heim Translation Fund Grant for her translation of Kazuki Kaneshiro's *GO.* Her most recent translation, "Mummy" by Banana Yoshimoto, appears in the anthology *The Book of Tokyo: A City in Short Fiction.* Her translations have also been published in *Words Without Borders* and *Asymptote.* She teaches at Sophia University in Tokyo.

Charles Patrick Norman has won several awards from PEN America, most recently third place in the 2015 Prison Writing Contest for Poetry. During his incarceration, his poetry, short stories and memoirs have garnered accolades from the Tampa Writers Alliance and the Ed Hirschberg Writers' Alliance, among others.

Suzanne Nossel is the executive director of PEN America. She served as executive director of Amnesty International USA, and she is the author of *Presumed Equal: What America's Top Women Lawyers Really Think About Their Firms*. Nossel has served as a senior fellow at the Century Foundation, the Center for American Progress, and the Council on Foreign Relations.

Alissa Nutting is the author of the novel *Tampa*. Her fiction has appeared in *The Norton Introduction to Literature, Tin House, Bomb,* and *Conduit;* her essays have appeared in *Fence, The New York Times, O: The Oprah Magazine,* and *Elle,* among other publications.

Joyce Carol Oates has written numerous books, including her 2015 memoir *The Lost Landscape: A Writer's Coming of Age*. She has been a member of the American Academy of Arts and Letters since 1978. Her honors include the Commonwealth Award for Distinguished Service in Literature, the *Kenyon Review* Award for Literary Achievement, the National Humanities Medal, and the Norman Mailer Prize.

Alicia Ostriker was twice nominated for the National Book Award. Her books include *The Old Woman, the Tulip, and the Dog,* published in 2014. Ostriker was elected a chancellor of the Academy of American Poets in 2015. She is currently a professor at Rutgers University.

Miroslav Penkov is a novelist and short story writer. He is the recipient of the BBC International Short Story Award and *The Southern Review's* Eudora Welty Prize. His first book, *East of the West,* was a finalist for the 2012 William Saroyan International Prize for Writing and the Steven Turner Award for First Fiction by the Texas Institute of Letters. His debut novel, *Stork Mountain,* will be published this spring.

Willie Perdomo was a finalist for the National Book Critics Circle Award in poetry for *The Essential Hits of Shorty Bon Bon*. He is also the author of *Smoking Lovely,* winner of the PEN/Open Book Award, and *Where a Nickel Costs a Dime,* a finalist for the Poetry Society of America Norma Farber First Book Award. Perdomo teaches at Phillips Exeter Academy.

Jesselyn Radack is a writer, a former ethics advisor for the United States Department of Justice, and an advisor for ExposeFacts' Whistleblower & Source Protection Program (WHISPeR). She has been granted the Sam Adams Award for integrity in intelligence and the Hugh M. Hefner First Amendment Award. Her memoir, *Traitor: The Whistleblower and the "American Taliban,"* was published in 2012. Radack was featured in the 2014 documentary *Silenced*.

Adriana E. Ramírez won the 2015 PEN/Fusion Emerging Writers Prize for her manuscript *Dead Boys*. Ramírez is the author of two chapbooks, *The Swallows* and *Trusting in Imaginary Spaces*. She currently teaches at the University of Pittsburgh, where she co-runs the Steel City Slam.

Camille Rankine's first full-length collection, *Incorrect Merciful Impulses*, was published in January 2016. She is also the author of the chapbook *Slow Dance with Trip Wire*, winner of the Poetry Society of America's New York Chapbook Fellowship. Rankine is assistant director of the MFA program in creative writing at Manhattanville College.

Roger Reeves's poems have appeared in many publications, including *Best American Poetry, Poetry, Ploughshares*, and *American Poetry Review*. Among his honors are a Hodder Fellowship from Princeton University, a Whiting Award, and a Ruth Lilly Fellowship. *King Me*, his first collection, was published by Copper Canyon Press in 2013.

James Risen is a journalist for *The New York Times* and the author and co-author of several books, most recently *Pay Any Price: Greed, Power, and Endless War*, published in 2014. Risen is a two-time Pulitzer Prize winner for national reporting.

Jarod Roselló is a Cuban-American teacher, cartoonist, and writer. He is the founder and editor of Bien Vestido Press. Roselló's chapbook of fiction, *This is Not Where You Belong*, was published in 2012 by Aestel and Ancanthus. Roselló's debut graphic novel, *The Well-Dressed Bear Will (Never) Be Found*, was published in August 2015.

Joseph Roth (1894-1939) was a political journalist and novelist. He wrote numerous books, including *Job, Radetzky March*, and *The Emperor's Tomb*. In 2015 a new collection of his journalism, *The Hotel Years*, was published by New Directions.

Ira Silverberg is a senior editor at Simon & Schuster. His background in publishing includes working as an editorial director at Grove/Atlantic Press and of Serpent's Tail. He has served as director of literature of the National Endowments for the Arts. In 2013 he was awarded the Publishing Triangle Leadership Award. He teaches at Columbia University.

Edward Snowden is a computer expert. He worked for the CIA and as a contractor for the U.S. government, gaining international attention in 2013 when he exposed classified documents from the United States National Security Agency. He currently lives in asylum in Russia.

Juliana Spahr is a poet, critic, and editor. She has published eight books of poetry, including *Fuck You-Aloha-I Love You, Well Then There Now,* and *That Winter the Wolf Came,* released in 2015. She was the recipient of the 2009 O.B. Hardison Jr. Poetry Prize, and is an associate professor of English at Mills College.

Tom Stoppard received the 2015 PEN/Allen Foundation Literary Service Award, as well as four Tony Awards, and an Academy Award for his screenplay *Shakespeare in Love.* Other works include *Rosencrantz and Guildenstern Are Dead, Jumpers,* and *Rock 'n' Roll.* His most recent play, *The Hard Problem,* premiered in 2015 at the National Theatre in London.

Merritt Tierce was a finalist for the 2015 PEN/Robert W. Bingham Prize for her first book, *Love Me Back,* which also won the Texas Institute of Letters' debut fiction award and was named one of the ten best books of 2014 by the *Chicago Tribune.* Tierce received a Rona Jaffe Foundation Writers' Award in 2011, and is a 2013 National Book Foundation "5 Under 35" author.

TC Tolbert's works include *Gephyromania, Spirare,* and *Territories of Folding.* In 2015, he/she was selected as one of the New American Poets by the Poetry Society of America. He/she teaches in the Low Residency MFA Program at Oregon State University—Cascades.

Dorothy Tse is a fiction writer based in Hong Kong. She won the Hong Kong Biennial Award for Chinese Literature and Taiwan's Unitas New Fiction Writers' Award. Tse's first English-translated collection, *Snow and Shadow,* was published in 2014. She is an assistant professor of creative writing at Hong Kong Baptist University.

Aurora Venturini (1922-2015) was an Argentinian writer. In 1948, Jorge Luis Borges awarded her the Initiation Award (Premio Iniciación) for *El Solitario*. Following the Revolución Libertadora, she spent twenty-five years in exile in Paris, during which time the French government awarded her an Iron Cross for her translations of François Villon and Arthur Rimbaud. Her novel *Las primas* won the Premio Nueva Novela Página/12 and the Premio Otras Voces, Otros Ámbitos.

Abdourahman Waberi is an award-winning writer from Djibouti. He is the author of numerous works of fiction, including *In the United States of Africa, Passage of Tears,* and *Transit.* Waberi is also a regular literary critic for *Le Monde.* He teaches French, francophone studies, and creative writing at George Washington University.

Binyavanga Wainaina is the founding editor of *Kwani?,* a leading African literary magazine based in Kenya. He won the 2002 Caine Prize for African Writing, and he has written for *Vanity Fair, Granta,* and *The New York Times.* Wainaina directs the Chinua Achebe Center for African Writers and Artists at Bard College.

Eleanor Wilner's collections of poetry include *Tourist in Hell* and *The Girl with Bees in Her Hair.* Wilner has been honored with numerous awards, including a MacArthur Fellowship, a National Endowment for the Arts Fellowship, the Juniper Prize, and two Pushcart Prizes.

C.D. Wright (1949-2016) published more than a dozen books, including *One With Others,* which was nominated for the National Book Award and won the National Book Critics Circle Award in 2010. She was also awarded a Guggenheim Fellowship, a Whiting Award, a MacArthur Fellowship, and a Griffin Poetry Prize. In 2013, she was appointed a chancellor for the Academy of American Poets. Her most recent book, *ShallCross,* was published in 2016.

Kerry Young is writer-in-residence at the University of Sheffield, an honorary assistant professor in the School of English at the University of Nottingham, and honorary creative writing fellow at the University of Leicester. Young is currently completing a trilogy of novels; the second installment, *Gloria,* was published in 2013.

ACKNOWLEDGMENTS

"The Pilot" by Russell Edson is reprinted from *The Tunnel: Selected Poems*, Oberlin College Press, 1994. Reprinted with permission from Oberlin College Press.

"Revulsion" by Horacio Castellanos Moya, is excerpted from *Revulsion: Thomas Bernhard in San Salvador*. Copyright © 1997 by Horacio Castellanos Moya. Copyright © 2016 by Lee Klein. Used by permission of New Directions Publishing Corp.

Many thanks to our colleagues at the PEN World Voices Festival, pen.org (especially the PEN Poetry Series and Guernica/PEN Flash Series), the PEN/HEIM Translation Grants and the PEN America programs for Literary Awards, Prison Writing and Free Expression.